Peacocks
on the Podium

Peacocks on the Podium

and other members of the musical menagerie

CHARLES NEILSON GATTEY

Hutchinson

London Melbourne Sydney Auckland Johannesburg

Hutchinson & Co. (Publishers) Ltd
An imprint of the Hutchinson Publishing Group
17–21 Conway Street, London W1P 6JD

Hutchinson Group (Australia) Pty Ltd
30–32 Cremorne Street, Richmond South, Victoria 3121
PO Box 151, Broadway, New South Wales 2007

Hutchinson Group (NZ) Ltd
32–34 View Road, PO Box 40-086, Glenfield, Auckland

Hutchinson Group (SA) Pty Ltd
PO Box 337, Bergvlei 2012, South Africa

First published 1982
Copyright © Charles Neilson Gattey 1982

Set in Times by Bookens, Saffron Walden, Essex

Printed in Great Britain by the Anchor Press Ltd
and bound by Wm Brendon & Son Ltd
both of Tiptree, Essex

British Library Cataloguing in Publication Data
Gattey, Charles Nielson
Peacocks on the podium.
1. Conducting (Music)—Anecdotes, facetiae,
satire, etc.
I. Title
781.6'35   MT85

ISBN 0-09-150870-3

Contents

Peter Pixis, the German pianist, whose huge nose Heine called 'one of the curiosities of the musical world', stayed once for two-and-a-half months at a hotel in Riga owned by a man named Langwitz, who loved music. When Pixis asked for his bill, he received the following:

75 portions of coffee and rolls	00,000
Dinners for 2½ months	00,00
49 bottles of wine	0,000
Tea, etc.	00
Lodging	000
Received with thanks – Karl Langwitz	

I dedicate this book to all other gifted music-makers, wishing them similar hospitality on their travels.

How to Live to a Ripe Old Age

It has been said that anyone wishing to live to a ripe old age should become an orchestral conductor. Sir Thomas Beecham died three weeks before his eighty-fifth birthday; Bruno Walter when he had reached that age; Toscanini in his ninetieth year, and Stokowski in his ninety-sixth. Sir Malcolm Sargent claimed that there was no more energetic occupation than conducting: 'I spend up to six hours a day waving my arms about and if everyone else did the same they would stay much healthier. When I'm not working, I put up my feet and relax.'

Sir John Barbirolli thought that perspiring was most beneficial to one's well-being and helped to keep down one's weight. A conductor once handed his 'little stick' weighing only half-an-ounce to a heavyweight boxer and challenged him to see for how long he could wave it about. After a very short while the boxer stopped, exhausted.

Apart from waving a baton, the playing of all types of musical instruments is, of course, bodily invigorating – even pedalling a pianola. Beverley Nichols in *The Unforgiving Minute* says that Professor Joad of BBC Brains Trust fame used to play Bach every morning on 'an odd sort of pianola contrivance, not because he was particularly enamoured of the fugues, but because the exercise of pedalling was good for his constipation'.

In ancient Egypt, a musician would beat time for the others by clapping his hands; in Greece, he stamped in a heavy leaden shoe; in Western Europe, in the Middle Ages, a monk would conduct a choir with a roll of parchment; whilst in the seventeenth century Jean-Baptiste Lully, King Louis XIV's leading court musician, used a staff to beat time on the wooden floor of a rostrum which acted as sounding-board. One day while directing the *Te Deum*, he accidentally crushed his big toe with it. The wound developed gangrene, from which he died.

There had been so many complaints about the din made by the thud of the stick that, after Lully's death, the practice ceased and soon it was discovered that one could conduct just as well with a stick half the length that need cause neither noise nor risk of accident. It was still held upright by both hands with thumbs pointing upwards, but lateral movement now became possible to achieve with ease as well.

The modern baton first came into fashion on the continent of Europe in the early nineteenth century. In 1810 Daniel Türk in Halle used to fling himself about so vigorously with his that, on several occasions, he shattered the chandelier above his head.

Ludwig Spohr claimed that he introduced the baton to England when he was a 'guest' conductor at concerts held in London in 1820 by the Philharmonic Society. He wrote later in his autobiography that, on arrival, he discussed his proposed innovation with the directors of the Society, and it was only after much argument that they allowed him to experiment at a rehearsal. He says: 'I could not only give the *tempi* in a very decisive manner, but indicate also to the wind instruments and horns all the entries which inspired them to play with a confidence such as they had never before known.' As a result, the orchestra unanimously agreed to this new way of conducting and the directors withdrew all further opposition.

Spohr goes on to say that his success on the evening of the concert itself was far greater than he could have hoped for. 'It is true that the audience was at first startled by the novelty and some were to be seen whispering among themselves. But when the music began, and the orchestra attacked the well-known symphony with unwonted force and precision, the prolonged applause after the first movement proved that there was general approval. The victory of the baton as a time-giver was complete.'

The change was, in fact, adopted only gradually. Sir George Smart, for example, five years later, at an important concert of the Philharmonic Society, sat as formerly at a piano and controlled the orchestra when necessary by use of the keyboard and occasionally a wave of the hand. Mendelssohn conducted with a baton at his Gewandhaus concerts in Leipzig, and when he visited London in May, 1829, to direct the Philharmonic he wrote next day to his parents: 'I mounted the rostrum and pulled out my white stick, which I have had made on purpose (the maker took me for an alderman, and would insist on decorating it ith a crown).'

From now on, the new fashion caught on so widely that in 1836 we find Robert Schumann in the *Neue Zeitschrift für Musik* complaining about 'the vanity and self-importance of the conductors' employing batons 'partly because they want to be constantly before the audience, partly to hide the fact that a competent orchestra can take care of itself without their leadership'.

Half a century on, Sarasate, the popular Spanish violinist, was to express similar disapproval when he met Granados. 'Enrique, do you know what is happening today?' he asked. 'I mean these conductors with their little sticks. They don't play, you know. They stand in front of the orchestra – and they get paid well, too. Now suppose, Enrique, suppose there were no orchestra and they stood there alone. Would they pay them just the same – them and their little sticks?'

Father of the 'Proms'

The first of the great 'show' conductors were Strauss in Vienna, Musard in Paris and Jullien in England. Born two years before the battle of Waterloo, in south-eastern France, he was christened Louis George Maurice Adolphe Roch Albert Abel Antonio Alexandre Noé Jean Lucien Daniel Eugène Joseph-le-brun Joseph-Barême Thomas Thomas Thomas-Thomas Pierre-Cerbon Pierre-Maurel Barthélemi Artus Alphonse Bertrand Dieudonné Emmanuel Josué Vincent Luc Michel Jules-de-la-plane Jules-Bazin Julio César Jullien after his thirty-six godfathers from the Philharmonic Society of Sisteron. Adept in the art of publicity, Jullien told journalists at the height of his career fanciful stories of his early days, such as that when a child the sound of music made him scream and foam at the mouth, which medical experts discovered was due to ultra-sensitive auricular organs and which had been cured by making him listen to Mozart's works at a distance from which most people would be unable to hear them.

Jullien claimed that at about the age of three he developed a beautiful singing voice and was regarded as an infant prodigy until, a few years later, he was snatched into the air by an eagle and on falling found he could no longer sing, so he took up the violin and might have become a second Paganini had he not been wounded in the right shoulder in 1827 whilst serving in the French navy. Next he went to Paris where, after working as a waiter or a cook, he studied music at the Conservatoire for a time until, through becoming friendly with Rossini, he was appointed chief of the orchestra for the balls held at the Jardin turc, where his personal magnetism and style of conducting drew large gatherings. We find the *Musical World* for 5 August 1836 reporting that he had become Musard's rival as a showman.

Whereas the former Musard contrived to smash the chairs, to fire off pistols, etc., for the purpose of giving éclat to his quadrilles, his praiseworthy ingenuity has been overwhelmed by his antagonist, Mons. Jullien conceived the happy idea of setting fire to the four quarters of the garden, in the midst of which is heard the discharge of musketry and the clanging of alarm bells; all of which is grounded upon motives from the *Huguenots*, Meyerbeer's opera.

Jullien was now living beyond his means and to avoid his creditors fled to London, where he originated the idea of holding cheap concerts for those who otherwise would spend their leisure in the galleries of theatres or public houses. For nearly nineteen years from 1841, he held what were in fact the first promenade concerts, chiefly at the Lyceum, Drury Lane and Covent Garden, usually with three hundred instrumentalists. Of the early *concerts d'été* at Drury Lane, the *Musical World* wrote that they provided 'an agreeable promenade in hot weather' in a luxuriant setting of growing shrubs and flowers and 'with fountains throwing their sparkling waters among the gaslights'. He resorted to startling theatrical effects, such as a crystal curtain, red fire, exploding percussion caps, and a band concealed in the 'flies' echoing the louder band on the stage. Women always packed the dress circle for he regularly presented all who sat there with his portrait.

Jullien once said: 'To succeed as a musician in England you must either be a great genius or a great charlatan like me.' A handsome man, dressed like a dandy with long, crimped hair and waxed moustaches – an astonishing new fashion for England – he would stand on a podium carpeted in crimson, patterned in gold, an ornately carved, gilded music-stand before him and a chair behind, known as his 'throne', upholstered in rich velvet. At the close of each concert he would sink on this chair with studied prostration. But when, during the course of the evening, he directed one of his own quadrilles, he would spring up on to his 'throne' and conduct from there. Then, at the climax, jumping down again, he would either snatch a violin from the nearest player or take a piccolo from a pocket and accompany the orchestra in ecstasy.

His baton was of maple wood, 22 inches long, with two golden serpents, each diamond-eyed, writhing round it; later the baton was further adorned with more gold and seven diamonds, plus a brilliant. The critic of the *Morning Herald* wrote in 1850: 'It flies about with the restlessness of lightning and his attitudes while working up a climax, dallying with a diminuendo, or enumerating a staccato, were as explanatory as words and infinitely more prompt.'

The 'Mons', as *Punch* called Jullien, always had white gloves brought to him on a silver salver for him to put on before he commenced conducting, and when any work by Beethoven was imminent a flunkey would appear with a clean pair, for Jullien regarded the master as the greatest of composers, to whom proper reverence must be paid. A German imitator, according to the *Musical Times* of July, 1884, 'in order that the public may be more deeply impressed with the feeling of grief intended to be produced by the Funeral March in Beethoven's Eroica Symphony, wears black gloves while conducting this movement, after having worn white gloves during the preceding parts of the Symphony'.

When light music was played, Jullien never tired of adding new effects. For the elder Strauss's *Pot-Pourri le Bouquet des Dames* there were Chinese chimes, cracking of whips, firing of cannon, flourishing of trumpets, ringing of bells, the blowing of a post-horn and the singing of 'God Save the Queen' preceded by a sledge party and accompanied by a Coronation Procession.

In 1844, Jullien introduced the polka to England. The following year, among *Punch*'s cartoons satirizing the new craze, is one of him tearing his hair in dismay because of a report that Queen Victoria disapproved of the dance and had forbidden its perpetration in the royal ballroom.

All Jullien's seasons at Covent Garden ended with a *bal masqué*, for which the auditorium would be draped with canary-coloured silk, trimmed with crimson velvet and gold lace; and it was at that theatre on 1 November 1846 that he first presented his famous British Army Quadrilles, played by the massed bands of the Life Guards, the Royal Horse Guards, the Grenadier Guards and the Coldstream Guards as well as by his own orchestra, all in tiers on the stage facing an audience of some three thousand.

Father of the 'Proms'

Ever seeking something novel and spectacular with which to attract the populace, Jullien held *concerts monstres* in the Surrey Zoological Gardens with 300 instrumentalists on a covered platform, with space for up to 12,000 people between it and the home of the giraffes. When, at the end, the National Anthem was played, cannon shots were fired after each bar. The playing of Beethoven's Battle Symphony was the highlight of the second *concert monstre*, and in order to heighten the effect of the war-like sounds Jullien added to the battery of instruments the largest bass drum ever seen or heard in Britain. For the *concert monstre* of 1849, the orchestra's strength was increased to 400 players supported by three military bands and three choirs and a galaxy of soloists. Those living in the vicinity claimed that they heard elephants vociferating in protest, but the sound came from some 29-foot-long trumpets hotting up the opening of a new Roman march.

On 17 August 1852 Jullien presented at Covent Garden a grand opera, *Pietro il grande*, with a score composed by himself, which was the most lavish production ever seen in England. There were three military bands, one mounted, and a small regiment of cavalry. Scenery, costumes and properties alone cost the equivalent of £250,000 today. Mauled by the critics, the opera's run lasted only five nights. According to the *Illustrated London News*, it was an 'unequivocal failure' and never had so much noise been heard before in an opera. Later, Jullien became obsessed by the belief that Meyerbeer had been present in disguise every night during the short run and had stolen the whole score for that of his own opera *The Star of the North*.

Rendered almost bankrupt by this disaster, Jullien decided to seek financial rehabilitation in the United States, where Barnum the previous year had made a fortune promoting Jenny Lind's concerts. On 29 August 1853 the 'Mons' opened in the Castle Garden, a former fort that the 'King of Humbug' had converted into a concert hall for Jenny's American début, and here Jullien bewitched the capacity audience of over 10,000 and had an equally triumphant reception. The *New York Tribune* wrote: 'He is a man not only of talent but of genius. . . . It must popularize musical art. It must elevate its standards. It must mend the morals

7

and manners of the people. While they learn to enjoy such music, they will not seek the more animal excitement of intemperance; they will not grow worse but better.'

The 'Mons' had rented Castle Garden for a month, and so great was the demand for tickets that he moved to the Metropolitan Hall for a further four weeks. New Yorkers previously apathetic to music's charms were attracted inside by the visual effects. When the orchestra played 'The Railroad Gallop', a model locomotive would puff round the stage on rails with clouds of 'smoke' rising from its funnels. Then, for 'The Fireman's Quadrille', red-shirted firemen stood with their hoses spraying water on a mock fire. Audiences were fascinated by the monster drum, the 15-foot-tall double-bass, the out-size octobass, the strange serpentcleide, bombardon and clavicor. A reporter wrote of 'a wonderful E pluribus *unum*, made up of a vast number of all sorts of drums, including *spare* drums, *side* drums, *bass* drums, humdrums and doldrums'. There were also 'four glorious gongs' and Jullien's 'famous desk, dressed in scarlet and supported by a pensive seraph petrified into well-chased gold'.

After touring the USA and giving a total of 214 concerts, Jullien returned to London, where he lost the money he had made in ill-fated ventures. Yet another blow befell him when the Covent Garden opera house was destroyed by fire in 1856 and he lost all his orchestral parts, including the only score in existence of his opera about Peter the Great.

For a while Jullien became interested in the idea of setting the Lord's Prayer to music, attracted by the prospect of having printed on the music sheets: 'Words by Jesus Christ, music by Louis Jullien.' But nothing came of it and in 1860, after being imprisoned for debt in Paris, he died there in an asylum.

Berlioz, who knew him well, had been aware of his worsening mental state and wrote in his memoirs:

For some years he had been laying claim to a remarkable discovery in the field of acoustics, which he eagerly imparted to everyone he met. He would place his fingers in his ears and listen to the dull roar produced by the blood passing through the carotid arteries and firmly believe that he was hearing the cosmic A given out by the terrestrial globe in its revolutions through space. He would then whistle through his lips some shrill note – a D, an E flat, or an F – and explain with the utmost enthusiasm, "Listen it's the A, the genuine A of the spheres! The vibrations of eternity!"

Sir Georges Groves has written that whilst Jullien was a public amuser, he was also a public reformer, and W.A. Davison, editor of the *Musical World* and music critic of *The Times*, maintained that he 'created a new taste for music among the middle classes'. The *Illustrated London News* agreed, stating:

His earliest concerts consisted almost entirely of showy and brilliant dance music to catch the most uncultivated ear. But he began to mingle this familiar music with things of a higher order: movements (short at first) from the symphonies of Haydn, Mozart or Beethoven. . . these innovations were often received by the denizens of the promenade with loud (and somewhat riotous) disapprobation. But still Jullien went on gradually increasing the wholesome doses, till his treatment of the patient (the public) at length prevailed; and he has left behind a name which will live in our musical annals as the name of a distinguished man, who has done as much as ever has been done by any single individual in promoting the progress of his art in this country.

JULLIEN'S DESPAIR

Podium Histrionics

Ernest Newman in the *Sunday Times* for 27 June 1948 wrote that he had received letters from 'hysterical women' asking indignantly why he had failed to praise a certain English conductor, who, as one lady put it, 'communicates his magnetism' to not only the orchestra but the audience as well. He had found the belief prevalent among the unmusical that conducting was a matter of magnetism which threw the orchestra into 'a catalyptic state in which, poor earthy clods as they would be if left to themselves, they utter Delphic oracles by the direct inspiration of this or that Apollo of the baton'.

Newman claimed that one of his most treasured letters came from a man asking for assistance in arranging some conducting experience for him. The applicant had never done anything of the kind, nor could he read a score, but had modestly concluded: 'I am conscious of possessing magnetism.' This aspirant to the podium can perhaps be excused from assuming that magnetism was such a key to success for, as we shall see later, this is the word that keeps on occurring in accounts of celebrated conductors.

A Spanish wonder man's agent had sent Newman some 'thrilling' facts about his client, mentioning that he had given a piano recital at the age of eight, had then become a bull-fighter in his spare time, which occupation he had abandoned at eighteen for the role of a conductor, and was now 'idolized by millions' and 'has 1,500 letters every week from fans, mostly women'.

In his article, which appeared the following Sunday, Newman wrote that the non-musical regarded the conductor as a combination of the hypnotist and the lion-tamer. That was not how

10

the orchestral players saw him; apart from a half-a-dozen or so of great conductors, they considered him 'a man doing the easiest of musical jobs and not always doing it dazzlingly well'. Newman quoted the stories of the instrumentalist who could not tell an enquirer who had conducted that evening's concert because he had 'forgotten to look'; and of the eminent concert soloist who had taken up conducting and, when asked how he had enjoyed the experience, replied that he hadn't because it was too easy compared with playing his instrument. A member of the London Symphony Orchestra questioned about 'that talented boy from Italy' had replied ambiguously: 'He's certainly the best conductor we've had this season.'

Ham acting in the legitimate theatre may almost have ended with the Victorian era, but conductors falling victim to the promptings of their egos have gone on indulging in orgies of gesticulation in order to attract attention and hoping to be regarded with awe and admiration by the public.

Take this extract from a review in the *Musical Times* of February, 1921, of Václav Talich's conducting at a Philharmonic Society concert in London:

M. Talich is one of those gentlemen who are so anxious to show why they have been brought all the way from the Rhine or the Vistula that they will spend a large part of the evening giving anything but the best. Emotions of anger, suffering and exaltation seem to convulse their arms, shoulders and heads, the outward sign, no doubt, of a last despairing attempt to communicate the eloquence that, for want of a common tongue, they have failed to put across at rehearsal. Meanwhile the most careful watcher cannot make out precisely what the conductor wants the orchestra to do.

And of Efrem Kurtz, in a London newspaper of August, 1937, a critic said:

Musical director Kurtz may not be the world's tallest conductor, but surely he has the longest reach. And that emphatic left hand! It lifts flowing streams from the 'cellos; it reaches out to pluck rich arpeggios from the harp. It blesses the first violins or suddenly whips round with a stop-me-and-buy-one signal to the percussion. For the oboe-cor anglais duet in the third movement of the 'Symphonie Fantastique' he seems to lift the instrumentalists up by their hair.

Alfred Hertz, who conducted German operas at the Metropolitan Opera, New York, in the first decade of this century, threw himself about with such forceful gestures that he had to change collar and shirt after every act. When the house lights were lowered and the members of the orchestra ceased tuning their instruments, he would always delay his appearance long enough to arouse apprehension in the audience that something might be amiss, with the result that when at last he arrived, they applauded more than usual in relief.

Tactful hints by the management failed to make Hertz give up this habit, even when a large note was put up in his dressing-room which read: 'Am I not always on time? Yes, I am not.' In some European opera houses, the orchestra pit had been completely concealed by a wooden hood so that attention should be concentrated on the stage and it was decided to do the same at the Met. Deprived of the audience's plaudits now that they could no longer see him, Hertz gave up delaying his entrance. The hood was eventually removed because it muffled the music, but it had served its purpose and Hertz never tried his old tricks again.

Gerald Jackson, the flautist, recalls that Paul Paray would give the off-beat 'with a twist of his backside instead of the baton'. His habit of dancing about the podium had led many times to his falling into the fiddles.

Some great conductors, Beethoven among them, react to the sounds of music as though they were possessed. At concerts, when seated at the piano, he would suddenly rise and conduct in a manner that gave orchestras nightmares. He regarded them as clay to mould as he desired. He was the first of the modern conductors, who, as Harold Schonberg has written in *The Great Conductors*, wanted 'to shape sound in a personal romantic manner, according to his inner vision'. Handicapped by his deafness, he never achieved that as a conductor, but he was 'the pioneer, the prototype'.

Schindler, Beethoven's secretary, wrote: 'He had ears only for his composition and was ceaselessly occupied by what gestures he could employ to indicate the desired expression. To suggest a *diminuendo*, he would crouch lower and lower, and at a *pianissimo* he would almost creep under the desk. When the volume of sound grew, he rose up as if out of a stage-trap until he stood upon the tips of his toes almost as big as a giant, waving his arms and as if about to soar upwards to the skies.' Spohr says that he often shouted, too, in order to contribute to the *forte*, without being aware of it.

Seyfried, the Viennese opera composer, has described what he witnessed at Beethoven's concert in the Theater-an-der-Wien on 8 December 1813. The maestro was playing a new piano concerto and at the first *tutti* forgot that he was a soloist and began to conduct. At the first *sforzando* he threw out his arms so vehemently that he knocked both candlesticks off the music rack on the piano. The audience burst out laughing, which so incensed him that he made the orchestra start all over again. To guard against a repetition of the accident, two boys from the chorus were told to stand on either side of Beethoven holding the lights in their hands. One of them came close to the keyboard and peered at the score. Then, when the *sforzando* was once more reached, the composer flung out his right hand giving the unfortunate boy such a blow on his mouth that he reeled and dropped the candlestick on the floor.

The other boy had kept a wary eye on the maestro and managed to duck and escape injury. This time, the audience laughed so heartily that Beethoven swelled with fury and broke half a dozen piano strings playing the first chord of his solo.

As Adam Carse has written, Beethoven had enough music in him to have made scores of conductors, but, quite apart from his growing deafness, he had neither the temperament nor the right personality for such work. Nevertheless, the bad conducting of a great man is always more interesting than the good conducting of a small man.

Spontini–Berlioz–Bülow–Richter

Beethoven's contemporary, Gasparo Spontini (1774–1851), was probably the most flamboyant of German conductors and certainly the most conceited. Frederick William III of Prussia engaged this son of Italian peasants to restore the languishing Berlin Opera and the tactics he employed led to his being called the Napoleon of the North. Unlike the little Corsican, however, he was very tall, with the bearing of an aristocrat, and when he stood on the podium his dark, moss-green jacket was festooned with row on row of orders and decorations. For a baton he used an ebony cosh with a solid ivory ball at each end, grasped in the middle, and his military-style commands were given in an odd mixture of German, French and Italian. When beginning, he would thunder: '*Allez! En avant! Martelez!*' and after the final rehearsal he would bid his men: '*Au revoir au champ de bataille!*'

All Spontini's contemporaries mention his compelling personality. Moritz Hanemann, the Berlin musician, wrote: 'Like a king, he strode onto the stage and taking up his field-marshal's position, he looked round with his piercing eyes, fixing them on the heavy artillery – that is what he called the cellos and basses – and then gave the signal to begin. . . . He stood like a bronze statue, moving only the lower part of his arm.'

When Spontini conducted his own opera, *La Vestale*, in Dresden, he boasted to Wagner that he could direct the orchestra with his eyes and really needed no baton. 'My left eye is trained on the first violins, my right on the second violins, and if the eye is to have power, one must not wear glasses, as so many bad conductors do, even if one is shortsighted like I am. . . . Confidentially, I cannot see as far as the length of my baton in front of me. But all the same I can make the troops play as I want, merely by fixing them with my eyes.'

Following a visit to Spontini in 1837, Clara Novello recorded her impressions: 'His house was a gallery of portraits of himself, alternating with sonnets in his praise, etc., all the way to his own sort of throne room, where he sat on a raised dais on an armchair with his portraits, busts, medals and sonnets all around him.'

Hector Berlioz (1803–69) has been described as the greatest virtuoso conductor of all time. Instruments had never sounded before as they were made to sound by Berlioz. When Ernest Legouvé saw him for the first time conducting a rehearsal of *Der Freischütz*, he described him as a young man 'trembling with passion' and with a head of hair that looked 'like an immense umbrella, projecting like a movable awning over the beak of a bird of prey'. It was 'both comical and diabolical at the same time'. Elsewhere, Legouvé wrote that Berlioz's hair resembled 'the edge of a precipice'. It gave him vertigo.

In 1840 Berlioz caused a sensation in Paris when he conducted with a drawn sword his *Symphonie funèbre et triomphale* in the open air, with a full orchestra and a military brass band of two hundred musicians; when it was over he lay stretched out across the kettle-drums weeping.

A German conductor, employing similar methods to Musard in Paris and Jullien in London, was Carl Wilhelm Ferdinand Guhr, who, in Frankfurt, when directing Haydn's *Creation*, reinforced the orchestra with military bands and at the words, 'Let there be light', arranged for all the gas jets in the auditorium to be fully raised.

Hans von Bülow (1830–94), first husband of Liszt's daughter Cosima, whose affair with Wagner led to a divorce, was told by César Cui, the Russian impresario: 'You don't shave, but you always have a razor in your mouth.' Brahms said of him: 'His praise smarts in the eyes like salt, so that the tears run.' Bülow flailed a trombone player with 'Your tone sounds like roast beef gravy running through a sewer' – and a tenor in *Lohengrin* with 'You are not a knight of the swan [Schwan] but of the swine [Schweis].'

An oft-quoted saying of von Bülow's is 'A tenor is not a man but a disease'. On hearing that a certain critic's praise could be assured through having cut-price music lessons from him, von Bülow commented: 'That's not too bad. He charges such small fees you might almost call him incorruptible.' Even those who admired von Bülow received no thanks from him. When presented by a committee with a laurel wreath in recognition of his talents, he snorted: 'I'm not a vegetarian.'

Equally disagreeable was the tyrannical Hungarian autocrat Hans Richter (1843–1916), former horn player, who made such an impression on the English musical scene as conductor of the Hallé concerts. 'He did not pose and gesticulate like a savage at a war dance.' wrote Bernard Shaw. However, towards the end of his long dictatorship in Manchester Richter became very unpopular because, as Gerald Cumberland wrote in *Set Down in Malice*:

He refused to recognize that there was any other than Teutonic music in the world. His intellect had stopped at Wagner. At middle age his mind had suddenly become set and he looked with contempt at all Italian and French music. . . . He hated those privileged to attend his rehearsals. He declared, quite unwarrantably, that we talked and disturbed him. But he never appeared to be in the least disturbed by the handful of weary women who with long brushes, swept the seats and the floor of the hall, raising whirlpools of dust fantastically here and there and banging doors in beautiful disregard of the Venusberg music. . .

Despite his long sojourn in England, never mastering the language, Richter would ask for sound to 'varnish' into the distance, and once, noticing some empty chairs in the orchestra, exclaimed: 'I see several who is not here.' Concerned that one of his instrumentalists might become an alcoholic, he confided to a friend: 'All day he quaff and quaff, then when evening comes, he cannot.' On another occasion, he requested from the clerk in the railway booking-office two tickets: 'Von for me to come back and von vor my vife not to come back.'

Nikisch–Mahler–Strauss–Weingartner

Twelve years older than Richter, and having first been a violinist, Arthur Nikisch (1855–1922) owed his success as a 'show' conductor to his personal charm. Even-tempered, ever polite, paternally regal in appearance, he was so well loved by orchestras that there was nothing they would not try their best to do for him. Fritz Busch, when with the Colonne, fell under Nikisch's spell the moment he came to them as a 'guest' conductor. Making his way to the podium, he beamed so benevolently at the players that all burst spontaneously into enthusiastic applause. Slowly removing his gloves, he assured them that it had been the dream of his life to direct so renowned a band of musicians. Though they did not know it, he said the same to all orchestras. Then his searching gaze lighted on an old viola player and he exclaimed: 'Schulze, old friend, what a wonderful surprise! I had no idea you had landed in this beautiful city. Do you remember how we played the Berg symphony under Liszt at Magdeburg?'

Busch adds that the viola player, of course, remembered and told the others afterwards that for this conductor he would use the entire length of his bow instead of the half he gave others. 'The born "guest" conductor, an improviser of genius,' Fritz called Nikisch, who hardly moved his baton, with its pear-shaped handle, and never made a superfluous movement. Whenever he made a bigger beat than usual or suddenly changed his facial expression and gesture, there would be an instantaneous response from the players. Sir Henry Wood, who resembled Nikisch in appearance, wrote that he 'almost hypnotized his orchestras', whilst a member of the London Symphony Orchestra once declared: 'Nikisch simply *looked* at us, often scarcely moving his baton, and we played as though possessed.'

Nikisch refused to regard composers' scores as sacrosanct. When interviewed by a journalist in Berlin in 1907, he defended the revising of Beethoven's symphonies on the grounds that instruments invented since his time could achieve what the primitive ones then in use could not. He also maintained that conductors were justified and often compelled to depart from Beethoven's instructions with regard to tempo and expression in order to bring out the maestro's real intentions. 'If one were, for example, to conduct the first movement of the Ninth Symphony exactly following his instructions, then this magnificent music would be rendered unbearable.'

Immensely gifted as he was, Nikisch disliked settling down to routine, plodding work and often did not look at a new score before the first rehearsal. On one occasion he arrived to rehearse a composition by Max Reger who, mischievously, suggested playing the final fugue. Nikisch assented and began going through the score. He could not find the fugue and asked Reger: 'Where on earth is it?' The reply came: 'There is none!'

Gustav Mahler (1890–1911) was a perfectionist who never 1860 found an orchestra of which he fully approved. It was he who said: 'Tradition is really just complacency and slackness.' On commencing his career as a conductor in Vienna he was so keen that he literally raced to the podium at every performance, according to the critic Max Graf. 'He would let his baton shoot forward suddenly, like a tongue of a poisonous snake. With his right hand, he seemed to pull the music out of the orchestra as if out of the bottom of a chest of drawers. If an instrumentalist made the tiniest error, he would shoot him such a venomous look that how ever far away the culprit was he would quail.'

As time passed, Mahler's style changed. He became more relaxed and still, with a simpler beat. Bruno Walter recalled a performance of the *Sinfonia Domestica* by Richard Strauss when 'the contrast between the uproar of the orchestra and the

17

immovable attitude of him who had unleashed it made a most eerie impression.'

If Mahler raced to reach the podium, Richard Strauss (1864–1941) raced from the moment he unleashed the orchestra. His tempi grew increasingly faster as his career progressed until no other conductor could compare with him for speed. This made for brilliant showmanship that riveted the attention of audiences. Toscanini took 2 hours 2 minutes over the first act of *Parsifal*, Karl Muck's time was 1 hour 54 minutes, but Strauss beat both with 1 hour 35 minutes. Until Strauss conducted Beethoven's Ninth Symphony in 45 minutes at Siegfried Wagner's Memorial Concert, no one else had taken less than an hour over it. An amazed spectator close to him remarked that at the end his collar was still dry and there was not a single drop of perspiration on his face. Strauss achieved this using a tiny baton and with minute, precise beats. He had unconventional views regarding the function of the left hand: 'It ought to have nothing to do with conducting. Its proper place is in the waistcoat pocket, from which it should emerge to restrain, or to make some minor gesture, for which in any case a scarcely perceptible glance should suffice.'

Mahler's successor at the Vienna Opera, Felix Weingartner (1863–1942), was popular in England. When he first conducted in London, in April 1898, the *Musical Times* enthused with clichés – 'magnetic', 'a leader of men' and 'a poet among conductors'. It was a pleasure to watch his physical movements, combining 'the dignity and calm of Dr Hans Richter with the quick-silvery alertness of Mr Henry J. Wood'.

In Paris, Weingartner's reception was less ecstatic. Debussy thought he conducted the Pastoral Symphony with the care of 'a conscientious gardener', whilst Colette in 1903 wrote:

Tall, clean-shaven, and with the colourless complexion, suddenly turning crimson, of an enlightened Jesuit, Weingartner conducts with gestures that are magnificent or ridiculous. His coat-tails jump up with the feverish jerks of his arms or fly around to the rhythm of his hammering fists. In opening the floodgates of music, this German works himself up to a state of epilepsy.

Later in life, in keeping with that of many conductors, Weingartner's style became less energetic, as may be gathered from Sir Henry Wood's assessment of him: 'He has an amazing facility for conducting with the eyes. He seems to get everything he wants by that means.' Sir Neville Cardus, writing of him conducting the Hallé at the age of 76, wrote that his gestures were quiet: 'He is seldom disturbed from a calm physical balance; his laundry-bill probably disappoints those who attend to the weekly linen of most of the other conductors.'

Koussevitzky–Furtwängler–Karajan–Mehta

Sergei Koussevitzky (1874–1951), regarded as the greatest of all Russian conductors and for so many years resident conductor of the Boston Symphony, let his emotions take control throughout his career. He entreated, he urged. His baton vibrated with excitement, whilst his features turned deep red and a large vein throbbed in his forehead. During his latter years, audiences often feared that he would collapse with a fatal coronary before the concert was over.

Koussevitzky's style was in complete contrast to that of his contemporary, Fritz Reiner of Philadelphia, who, it was said, conducted as if balancing a toothpick on his baton's tip.

In common with the other 'show' conductors, Koussevitzky had that personal magnetism which, as Ernest Newman wrote, the non-musical have regarded as of vital importance in a conductor. One widow in her late sixties gushed: 'Even for me, he could be dangerous.' But those who worked with him were aware of his faults, such as losing his way in the score and cueing the wrong players – which they tolerantly disregarded without fuss.

He had an erratic beat, which puzzled the players when he became conductor at Boston. It is said that they conferred with one another and decided that when his hand passed the third button on his waistcoat that was the downbeat.

Leonard Bernstein has related how on another occasion the members of the orchestra nerved themselves to ask Koussevitzky himself for guidance. 'Ven my stick touches de air, you play,' he told them.

Bernstein comments that there was more in such a reply than might seem. 'When you want an ethereal sound, as at the beginning of the Prelude to *Lohengrin*, a downbeat would be almost too crude. The "stick touching the air" is really the effect you want.'

Koussevitzky was unable to communicate clearly with his players so that they knew at once precisely what he wanted. 'Eet mus' be more beautiful,' was one of his pet phrases, which did not tell them much. Still they would have another attempt, and he would start screaming until eventually, somehow, the playing did become more beautiful.

Conductors are not commonly regarded as shy men, but Wilhelm Furtwängler has surprisingly claimed that he had a successful career because he was awkward and shy, adding: 'My colleagues did not consider me dangerous as a result. When they finally realized that I was indeed a danger, it was too late.' His beat, like Koussevitzky's, mystified players. It seemed to be more like an attack of trembling. When he conducted for the first time at La Scala the leader of the orchestra, assuming this was due to nerves, leant forward and whispered, '*Coraggio, signore!*'

Sometimes mentioned as an example of his bewildering technique was Furtwängler's uncertain, quivering upbeat at the beginning of the Egmont Overture. The players had to decide for themselves when the baton would cease jittering and they could commence playing. A journalist once asked a member of the Berlin Philharmonic: 'How do you know when to come in on the opening bars of the Beethoven Ninth?' The reply given was: 'We walk twice round our chairs and then count ten.' Another reporter enquired: 'How do you know when to come in with such a peculiar downbeat?' and the answer this time was: 'When we lose patience.'

Furtwängler was aware of the orchestra's feelings, and on one occasion he paused during a rehearsal and told them: 'You believe that I'm unable to give you a conventional beat. I will now do so.' However, after a short while, he gave it up, making the excuse: 'But it has no quality.'

Players found that the best guide to Furtwängler's intentions was to study his facial expressions. He lacked the ability to make himself understood when speaking. Gregor Piatigorsky quotes him as saying: 'Gentlemen, this phrase must be – it must – it must – you know what I mean – please try it again – please.' Later, delighted with how the rehearsal had gone, he told Piatigorsky loftily: 'You see how important it is for a conductor to convey his wishes clearly.'

Furtwängler became increasingly deaf as he grew older. Eventually the podium had to be wired to enable him to hear the orchestra. He also developed an annoying habit of having the players repeat musical phrases until they were exhausted. He became obsessed with the belief that rivals were plotting to oust him, his particular *bête-noir* being Herbert von Karajan.

As conductor of the Berlin Philharmonic following Furtwängler's death, Karajan, unlike his predecessor, avoided all unnecessary movement, kept his features practically impassive, whilst his arms stroked the air with meaningful grace. James Galway, who for a time was principal flautist under Karajan, claimed: 'Something happens when he comes on the platform that happens with no other conductor.'

Paul Robinson in his book on Karajan has written that there are those who say that the Berlin Philharmonic is incomparable, but that behind all Karajan's virtuosity there is nothing, because he is obsessed with the manipulation of sound. That was not Robinson's impression: 'Karajan is not invisible and if that's what people expect of a conductor then Karajan is not their man. To bring Beethoven's blazing vision to life in performance requires a force of personality no less blazing. And Karajan has a unique capacity for drawing from the hundred or so orchestra members everything they have in terms of both technique and feeling.'

Adverse criticism has come in the United States from Winthrop Sargeant, who wrote in 1961 of Karajan's *Tosca*: 'It's like having a good, simple, rare hamburger for a change. The amount of energy you can expend in *Tosca* – why it corresponds to a murder and the beauty of it is that you don't have to be hanged afterwards.'

And of the Bach concerts Karajan conducted with the Berlin Philharmonic at the Carnegie Hall in 1967, the same critic wrote: 'Mr von Karajan's duties seemed to be to wave a hand occasionally at the group, to plunk out the *continuo* at the second harpsichord, and to turn pages for Miss Bilgram. Otherwise, he was a mere ornament, though, to be sure, Mr von Karajan is unquestionably ornamental.'

Then, eight years later, Stephanie von Buchan declared in *Musical America*, regarding the maestro's conducting at a New

York concert: 'He ruined the Beethoven Fourth by offering a mannered, brutal reading that sounded as if it had been designed to get through to Beethoven a year after he went deaf.'

Karajan has made films of *La Bohème, Carmen* and *Pagliacci*, in which he also acted bit parts in various hirsute disguises. His showmanship is most noticeable in his concert films. Paul Robinson describes one of them as follows:

In the Beethoven Ninth, one sees little except violin bows, bells of trumpets, and the like, but above all, Karajan himself, eyes closed, making beautiful gestures. It is as if the members of the orchestra ceased to exist and the music was created by Karajan and a hundred instruments. . . . Truly an example of Karajan's narcissism in its most objectionable form. Yet, in other respects, there is clearly an attempt to provide a viable visual counterpoint to the musical substance which is the fundamental problem of showing music on films. Karajan has sought to avoid shots of horn players emptying the saliva from their instruments or of players appearing inactive while performing.

The adjective most commonly applied to describe Karajan's gestures is 'graceful'. One of its antonyms would be more suitable in the case of Sir Georg Solti, whom Harold C. Schonberg described in the *New York Times* for 28 November 1976 as 'the least graceful conductor since Dimitri Mitropoulos' and continued: 'His motions are jittery; his whole body is in motion; his shoulders as well as his hands are responding to the rhythm; his beat is a series of jabs, and he looks as though he is shadow boxing.'

There is a saying that in conducting a clear gesture is worth a thousand words. Zubin Mehta, the Parsee violinist, who became the colourful and dynamic conductor of the Los Angeles and the New York Philharmonic Orchestras, was taught the art in Vienna by Professor Hans Swarowsky, disciple of Richard Strauss, who cured his pupil's inclination to over-conduct with flailing arms by seizing them from behind, leaving only his wrists free, and then saying: 'Now you conduct.' Picking up the score, he went on:

This is your Bible or your Koran or whatever it is where you come from. You will adhere to this completely. In here you will find everything there is to know. . . When you make a *rubato*, when you take a liberty of any kind, you had better find something in here that told you to do that. Because if you do something that is not written in this book, then you have broken all Ten Commandments at once.

It was a lesson that Zubin never forgot, though he failed to conquer one fault – standing with his feet far apart when conducting, despite the Professor's constant exhortations that he should keep them together. The many years Mehta has spent in Los Angeles have resulted in his becoming very much of a showman. In 1964 a critic complained that his visually arresting style was designed to conduct the audience, whilst a member of the latter once said: 'One feels he's going to turn his hand into a claw and rip up the furniture, to show how powerful he is, and shout *Ecco il leone!* But he never does. He's just a lamb in a lion's skin.'

On 22 November 1977, the much-publicized 'Music From Outer Space' concert was staged in the Hollywood Bowl with Zubin Mehta directing the Los Angeles Philharmonic in a programme of music from the films *Star Wars* and *Close Encounters of the Third Kind*. An audience of some 18,000 was whipped up into a state of screaming hysteria by the music Mehta conducted to the accompaniment of fireworks and laser lights.

Toscanini–Mengelberg–Wood–Beecham

The greatest perfectionist of all conductors was Arturo Toscanini, who would never tolerate any performance that was not first-class. Once, as 'guest' conductor, he was rehearsing the *Eroica* symphony. The first and second movements were played through without any interruption from him and the orchestra were congratulating themselves that he must be satisfied. But it proved to be the hush before the hurricane that battered them after the scherzo. After furiously finding fault after fault with their performance, he staggered from the platform, vowing not to return until some six instrumentalists were replaced; and, despite the fact that every seat had been sold, the concert had to be postponed for five days so that this could be done to his satisfaction.

The 'Old Man', as he was called, treated any careless or inefficient playing as a personal affront. Though short-sighted, he could spot incorrect bow movements up to thirty feet away. 'Bah! I understand you make the mistake once, yes', he would exclaim: 'but I do not understand you make it a second time. *Santo Dio! Via, via, via!* Take care!'

Bernard Shore, who played first viola under him on many occasions, has recorded an admirably vivid description of the maestro's art in *The Orchestra Speaks*. The motif of every rehearsal was: '*Cantando, sempre cantando!* You must sing every note you play, sing, even through your rests. Not only play correctly – sing, *molto cantando*, all the time! Ah, *cantare, cantare!* Music, unless you sing, is nothing.' That one word, *cantando*, said Shore, expressed all Toscanini desired so intensely from his orchestra.

Up to 1897 in the famed Teatro Regio, Turin, the auditorium had remained fully lit during the performance so that people could do as they pleased – stroll about, chat to friends, eat and drink, play cards and make love; even some opera buffs approved of the illuminated auditorium, for it enabled them to follow better what was happening on the stage by reading the libretti. Toscanini considered darkness, except on the stage, essential in order to attain complete theatrical illusion. So as he mounted the podium in February that year for the first performance of *Tristan*, all the house lights went out. Pandemonium followed. There was an angry chorus of protesting shouts countered by approving cheers from the Wagnerites.

Toscanini was forced to cease conducting, and when the timorous management yielded to the old guard and the lights came on again, he smashed the lamp on his desk in a fury. After a battle of words, a temporary truce was reached and Toscanini reluctantly agreed to a compromise and the performance resumed with the auditorium half-lit. But, instead of standing, he sat sulking with his right hand on his knee, leaving Enrico Polo to lead the orchestra while the prompter had a busy time helping the singers.

It proved a hard struggle but eventually this dictator of the baton had his way. Earlier, in the 1870s, he had achieved another important improvement at the same theatre. There had been no pit and he believed that Wagner was right in saying that orchestras should be hidden from the audience, so Toscanini persuaded the management to do this. In a letter of 10 July 1871, to Ricordi, he wrote:

24

It seems impossible that in this day and age one still tolerates seeing our wretched frock-coats and white bow-ties, mixed together with an Egyptian, Assyrian or Druid costume, etc., etc., and furthermore, to see the orchestra, which is part of the fictitious world, almost in the middle of the ground floor, in the world of the hissers or applauders. Add to all this the obscenity of seeing the harpists' heads, the double bass players' cuffs and the conductor's windmill.

The year after the *Tristan* tussle at Turin, thanks to Toscanini, a new curtain was installed at La Scala which opened laterally instead of vertically because he considered it inartistic for the audience to see first singers' feet, then knees and waists, upwards. He also refused to conduct unless the women seated on the ground floor removed their hats and that the auditorium here, too, should be in complete darkness once the curtain rose.

When Toscanini went to conduct at the Metropolitan in the first decade of this century there were those who predicted a short stay owing to his temper, but fortunately the general manager, Gatti-Casazza, was a masterly diplomat, not easily ruffled, and for fourteen years the partnership survived. A wit once described it as 'the cohabitation of a tortoise with a cat'.

There was a stormy beginning, when Toscanini swore in Italian at the orchestra, accusing them of playing like pigs and calling them 'Assassins!' He shouted at a trumpet player: 'God tells one how the music should sound but you stand in the way!' When his remarks were translated into English, the players marched out declaring they would not play for him again until he apologized. One of the management went to parley with him. He refused to retract his words, insisting that every one was true. Eventually, he suggested a solution to the problem which brought peace: 'I go to rehearsal and smile and say, "Good morning".'

One artist at least was fair-minded enough not to take offence at the maestro's abuse. In 1915, at a rehearsal of Giordano's *Madame Sans-Gêne*, Toscanini shrieked at Giovanni Martinelli: 'You! You sing like – like a police dog!' The tenor merely smiled, and confided later to a friend: 'I said to myself "Maybe he's right!" '

But such restraint under fire was exceptional. Three years later, Toscanini conducted the first post-war concerts at La Scala. During a rehearsal with the orchestra of Beethoven's Ninth

Symphony, he suddenly rapped angrily on the desk with his baton and, turning to a second violin, demanded: 'What do you think you're doing, scratching away like that with only two centimetres of your bow?' And he hurled the crumpled handkerchief which he had been using to fan himself at the violinist, who replied: 'I'm playing, not scratching. And what do you mean by throwing your handkerchief at me?' Trembling with rage, Toscanini stepped down from the podium and went towards the man, shouting: 'I throw everything I have into what I'm doing, but you throw nothing – nothing, d'you hear?'

The violinist protested: 'I've always done my best, and you're very rude.'

'Your best! Why you haven't the faintest idea how to use that!' Toscanini sneered, knocking the bow from the man's hand. It broke and on the rebound hit the player on the forehead. He jumped up and glared at Toscanini. The other violinists threw themselves between the pair, then one of them led his sulking colleague away. As he left the stage, the violinist yelled at the conductor: 'You're no maestro – you're a bully!'

The next day Toscanini walked on to the stage, as if in a dream, mounted the podium, looked round at the whole orchestra preparatory to beginning the rehearsal. Then he noticed that the maligned second violinist was present, and suddenly stepping down he went over to him and shook his hand.

In 1928 when the New York Symphony was merged with the New York Philharmonic Orchestra and Toscanini was appointed principal conductor, some of the players who had never worked with him but were aware of his reputation were really scared. They knew that he was supposed to have broken more batons on his podium than any other conductor and had pummelled with his fists a careless reed player. Winthrop Sargeant, who was then a violinist with the New York Symphony, has written that his colleagues would show pictures of a scowling Toscanini to their children and warn that if they misbehaved he would punish them. Instrumentalists began taking their parts home and practising them.

'Each movement of a symphony became an emergency which demanded every ounce of energy and concentration if it were not to end in an overwhelming catastrophe. Each performance was played as though our very lives depended on its perfection. Beyond all technique there was a residue of mysterious personal power that lay outside ordinary comprehension.'

According to the string player Samuel Antal, when Toscanini flew into a rage: 'It was among the most horrifying sounds I have ever heard, and seemed to come from his entrails. He would almost double up, his mouth opened wide, his face red as if on the verge of an apoplectic fit. Then a raucous blast of unbelievable volume would blare forth.'

'*Cantare! Sostenare!*' Toscanini would keep urging at rehearsals, and, says Antal: 'No conductor could create such a feeling of ecstasy.'

Toscanini himself would have refuted any suggestion that he was an egoistic show conductor. Ogo Ojetti, correspondent for the *Corriere della sera*, reported him as saying in 1930 that the most important quality in a conductor was humility.

If something does not go well, it is because I have not understood the composer. It is all my fault. Whoever thinks that Mozart, Beethoven, Wagner, Verdi, are mistaken and have to be corrected is an idiot. They have not written music in order to make me feel good. It is I who must make them look good by revealing them as they are... The conductor must not create, he must achieve humility, faithfulness, clarity, unity.

A conductor Toscanini could not stand, because he was so garrulous, was Willem Mengelberg, celebrated for having made the Amsterdam Concertgebouw one of the most esteemed of European ensembles. Mengelberg resembled Grock the clown, and, although short and stout, had the essential personal magnetism of the 'show' conductor that made him appear to grow in stature once on the podium. Often he would conduct without a baton, joking that it had given him a bad corn on his hand. No matter how eminent the composer, he would change the score directions if he thought he knew better. Bernard Shore in *The Orchestra Speaks* tells how Mengelberg justified this:

Beethoven, like many other composers, made changements in his scores, even after publication, and then he also vos deaf. So vy not the conductor also, who often knows mooch better than the composer? I vos de best pupil

27

of Schidler, so I know vat Beethoven meant. Zo, in dis verk of Strauss, I haf been great friend of Richard Strauss, since I vos a boy, and I know joist what he vants, and ve will make some changements also!

Presumably Mengelberg was referring to Schindler, Beethoven's private secretary, when he said 'Schidler'. If so, he may have been fooling the orchestra, for Schindler died seven years before Mengelberg was born.

No other conductor can surely have talked so much at rehearsals as Mengelberg. He lectured the players on one occasion for one and a half hours, according to Carl Flesch, then they rehearsed the music for half that time.

Conductors have indulged in various devices to attract attention to their batons. Sir Eugene Goossens used an illuminated one for a scene performed in total darkness when he conducted *Hiawatha* in 1924 for the Royal Choral Society, whilst Sir Henry Wood himself painted his long white baton with two coats of matt finish paint because he wished it not to catch the light and to be easily seen by every member of the orchestra, which would give them no excuse for not watching it. 'Why don't you look at my stick?' he would chide. 'It's clear enough! Every morning I practise for half-an-hour in front of the mirror.' New and nervous recruits to his orchestra would be told not to worry: 'You may be reading at sight in public, but you can't possibly go wrong with *that* stick in front of you.'

According to the flautist Gerald Jackson, Sir Henry's baton in action appeared to be 'at least a yard long, and as it swished through the air you could hear every tempo coming in with the beat'. Wood's reason for such a length was because a short baton gave him neuritis whilst a long one saved arm movement and was more noticeable in a wide beat. These batons were made for him by Palmers of Yarmouth strictly in accordance with his instructions. The weight had to be a shade less than one ounce, the shaft's length nineteen inches, the handle's five inches. Only one person dared to take liberties with Sir Henry's batons. That was Dame Ethel Smythe, who, when she conducted a work of hers at a Prom, picked up his baton, broke it in two, flung away one half and used the other. She was, of course, a militant suffragette.

At the start of his career, Wood had taken Nikisch for his

sartorial model, so he affected a bow tie, a broad-brimmed hat and an overcoat with a grandduke's fur collar. This, together with his black gipsy-like hair and striking blue eyes, made him look very much the 'show' conductor. Later came a period when 'Old Timber', as he was affectionately dubbed, could not care less what he wore and people often wondered if he slept in his suit, the trousers of which were held up by outsize safety-pins. When asked why he always wore a black waistcoat with his evening dress, he said it was 'for reasons of economy'. In 1933 James Agate in the *Sunday Times* wrote that he noticed Wood was dressed in 'what, except for undertakers', must be the last frock-coat in London'. But four years later he suddenly started sprucing himself up. He took to white waistcoats, and had his hair, beard and moustache expertly trimmed. Boots he continued to wear because they gave him ankle support, which he claimed was 'essential to anyone so much on his feet as myself when conducting'.

A friend of mine attended a concert given in Bradford during the Second World War by the London Symphony Orchestra when the Mendelssohn Violin Concerto was performed with Ida Haendel as the soloist. Sir Henry appeared wearing ginger-coloured plus-fours and jacket, and told the audience: 'I must apologize for my unusual costume, but my other clothes are somewhere between here and London, or else Adolf Hitler has them.'

At the Queen's Hall, Wood proved a strict disciplinarian. Players accustomed to arrive from 10.30 am for rehearsals were at first dismayed to find themselves expected to be in their places by 10.00 am. On his desk he would have in a conspicuous position his huge turnip-shaped watch, which he boasted was more reliable than Big Ben. Anyone late would be greeted with 'What, another cab horse down?' Later, he was to explain that having been only 25 years of age when he became conductor there, some of the older players thought him an upstart; he had even overheard himself called 'a whipper-snapper', so he had decided not to give them an inch. 'I meant to be on top. Therefore it was necessary to begin on top.' But he became a benevolent despot.

J.P. O'Callaghan, who attended regularly the Queen's Hall concerts, has described certain somewhat theatrical mannerisms of Wood's in those days. He would raise his baton high above his head for the brass, give an emphatic double nod to the strings in unison passages – and would make a 'sensitive withdrawal, as if he had been stabbed, when a *pianissimo* was not *pianissimo* enough'. All this dramatization of the music exhilarated people and made them come again. Wood behaved, too, like a showman in his exploitation of Wagnerian percussion effects: deafening brass, floor-quaking timpani and booming drums.

Sir Henry's voice could be easily heard at rehearsals, no matter how far away he stood or how loudly the orchestra played. At the Royal College of Music he had been taught singing by the great Manuel Garcia who told him: 'You have a conductor's voice – it would go through a brick wall. Promise me you won't sing in public.' In fact Wood began his career as a teacher of singing, so as a conductor he would never hesitate to draw the attention of vocalists to their faulty breathing. Reginald Pound in his biography of Sir Henry wrote: 'Sometimes a singer, too obviously inhaling, would be halted with the startling reminder: "Not like a vacuum cleaner!" ' He considered 'tight throaty tenors' always a problem, and 'the hollow, cowlike megaphone tones of the average bass most objectionable'.

Bernard Shore in *The Orchestra Speaks* relates that once at the old Crystal Palace, when rehearsing a monster performance of Verdi's Requiem with a huge orchestra and chorus as well as two brass bands in the galleries at the far end of the transept, Sir Henry suddenly rang a large dinner-bell to stop everything. Then, he boomed through a megaphone at the chorus, which had been late with two or three entries: 'You're late because you *will* breathe through your noses! I don't want any nose-breathers here! Suck in air through your mouths.'

Even well-known singers were not spared Wood's forthright comments, Shore tells us, such as 'What are you doing? But, my dear lady, you are not holding your quaver, so your rhythm goes to pieces. I know what it is, you want to bottle me up, and I won't *be* bottled up.' And if the singer should hold up a rehearsal through failing to spend time preparing the piece beforehand, Wood would not hesitate to lecture the offender on 'knowing your job'.

Collin Brooks wrote in the *Devil's Decade* that the baton was Sir Henry Wood's sceptre and that he was almost guilty of making it a fetish. In contrast, Sir Thomas Beecham conducted by personal magnetism, using his baton more as a lightning rod than a metronome. As Brooks puts it: 'His methods had something of Svengali in them. What the Victorians called "the electric fluid" seemed to pour out of him: he hypnotized an orchestra of metaphorical Trilbies into doing his will. Something, so to speak, came out of his left shoulder or his right elbow. He conducted not with his baton but his daemon.'

Dr Ben Horsfall, leading violinist for many years, stressed how Beecham's presence was eloquent in itself and inspired players.

Never at any time could I escape his penetrating eyes. The baton was exclusively for audience entertainment: how very often he flicked it like a fan, cracked it like a whip, or slowly dipped it into some imaginary inkwell: all very confusing for the public. After pre-war Hallé concerts I was often accosted by bewildered members of the audience with the remark: 'I don't know how you follow him.' There was a simple answer – we didn't; we were *with* him, and memorably so.

Only 'Tommy' could have behaved as he did. Sir Neville Cardus, discussing how Beecham ignored all the rules and moved hands and body in every direction at the same time, also claimed: 'I have seen Beecham's baton fly from his grip high into the orchestra's Empyrean. I have seen it entangled in his coat tails.' Olin Downes, music critic of the *New York Times*, wrote in 1941:

He may run all around the conductor's stand, or lean over, his toes perilously near its edge, in favoring a group or the player of a solo passage, with his exclusive attention. He may crouch. . . ungracefully crook a knee, or stoop down and rise like a large and ungraceful bird flapping its wings in the air. He may indicate a *sforzando* in the manner of a man hurling a brick or a bomb at a foe, or beat the measure freely with one arm while holding the baton in a clenched fist invisible to the orchestra.

Sargent–Stokowski–Bernstein

'Sir Thomas Beecham became an almost permanent headline. Sir Henry Wood became a cult,' was Collin Brooks' brilliantly crisp summing up of the main difference between their respective careers. When it comes to comparing the latter with Sir Malcolm Sargent, then how better to portray this than by recalling that Wood would have a poached egg and half a glass of mineral water before conducting, whereas Sargent's snack would consist of oysters and champagne. Sir Malcolm was a master of tasteful and polished showmanship. He argued that it undoubtedly helped to heighten an audience's enjoyment of music, and that there was a deep-rooted desire for it in most human beings: artists with this rare talent should not be deterred from employing it through fear of ridicule by killjoy pedants who themselves were devoid of such a gift.

An excellent example of how Sargent, through consummate showmanship, turned a near-fiasco into a triumph occurred en route to the Brussels Exposition in 1958, when he and his orchestra stopped in Ostend to give a concert. Probably because so many Belgians were already away in their capital, bookings were poor, and Sargent broke this dismal news to the players at the close of rehearsals, adding: 'We know the music is first-class. The only thing that need worry us is if, by any chance, we don't give a first-class performance.'

About a hundred and fifty people were scattered about the large hall in the Kursaal that evening. When the interval was reached, Sargent thought of a plan to boost the orchestra's morale and enliven the audience, and told Paul Beard, his leader: 'At the end, I bow. Then I bring you up. I come back for a fourth call. You are still standing. I shake hands with you and the leaders all round. I go off. I come on again for my fifth call. I get hold of you by the hand and draw you off the stage.'

This inspired idea had the exact effect Sargent hoped it would. The tiny gathering thoroughly appreciated the *tour de force* of showmanship and responded with applause that sounded as if it came from ten times their number. After his fifth call, Sargent cleverly dragged Paul Beard off the platform in the manner of one thinking: 'Really, we can't stay here *all* night, even if these thousands want us to do so.'

Bernard Shore had vivid memories of Sargent as a young conductor with flying arms crashing with a breathless orchestra through a piece of his own, called 'Impressions of a Windy Day'. His stick moved so fast, says Shore, that 'it could scarcely be seen but seemed to make a blur like the spokes of a fast-moving wheel'. And all the time Sargent was rehearsing he never stopped talking.

In 1936, fulfilling an engagement as 'guest' conductor in Sydney, Sargent went for the first get-together wearing his customary red carnation in the buttonhole of his faultlessly-cut suit. The Australian instrumentalists gaped at him with incredulous amusement, for they had never seen a conductor thus adorned before when rehearsing. At the first break, the brass section went across to the Marble Bar for refreshment, passing as they did so by a barrow selling glossy red toffee-apples. When they returned, every man sported one of these in his button-hole. Sargent laughed as heartily as the orchestral players.

Another great showman was Leopold Stokowski (1882–1977), son of a Polish father and Irish mother. Born in London, he was conductor for a quarter of a century of the Philadelphia Orchestra, became internationally famous through the Hollywood films *One Hundred Men and a Girl* and *Fantasia*, and was thrice married – once to a Vanderbilt. He began controversially in Cincinatti, where the *Cleveland Leader* accused him of being a conductor 'who made Beethoven dance on his ear; who made Brahms a puling, sickly sentimentalist; who calcined Strauss in more clashing and fighting colors than Strauss ever knew; and who Stokowskized each composer whom he took into his dictatorial hands'. In Philadelphia the public were told, under the headline 'Stokowski Trains Like A Prize Fighter', that he had a room at the Academy of Music fitted out with hot and cold needle showers and a rubbing table upon which he would lie while a masseur worked over him before and after each concert. The press were encouraged to interview and photograph him resting beneath a sheet.

When over-strenuous baton beating gave him neuritis in the right shoulder, Stokowski first transferred his stick to the left hand and later ceased using it; instead, he would mould each musical phrase with his fingers. At the Metropolitan, New York, when Alban Berg's *Wozzeck* was presented, he arranged for the lighting to cast arresting shadows of the play of his hands on walls and ceilings. At Carnegie Hall concerts and elsewhere, a spotlight lent a silvery radiance to his hair and a beam of light was focussed on his fingers. He would play a clavichord with his left hand while conducting with the other, pioneered the colour organ with flashing lights, and made the front page through a 'gimmicky' production of *Oedipus* with Buffano's twenty-foot marionettes. When conducting *Lohengrin* at the Bolshoi, he used two floodlights. Every time good came close to victory the red one was switched on, then when evil was in the ascendant it went out and the blue one shone. Audiences adored him, whilst he intimidated the critics and upset the old school, such as Sibelius, who observed: 'He is a very fine man I am sure and interested in many things – but not, I think, in music.'

In more recent times musical showmanship has gone to some extremes and very often the publicists employed by promoters are to blame. In order to draw the public to the concerts, the conductor has to appear successfully on television. It was André Previn's clowning with Morecambe and Wise in their BBC Christmas Show that made him popular with the millions who had never set foot in the Festival Hall. 'They couldn't have given a damn about the Beethoven programme we'd done the week before,' Previn has commented, 'but now they thought, well, if this guy's a symphony conductor maybe we should go to a concert.' Later, as a result, when the London Symphony went on its annual tour all the concerts were sold out weeks in advance.

Leonard Bernstein was the first conductor to become a top television personality. On 14 November 1954, thanks to a calculated risk on the part of the Columbia Broadcasting Service of America, he gave a talk on Beethoven that lasted forty-five minutes. It proved an astonishing success. There was nothing professorial or upstage about his manner, which was lively and amusing and appealed to all classes and ages. Many admired the skill with which he sold his product, music, and women longed to have him in bed with them. A whole series of such 'Omnibus' lectures by him followed. Over a year later, on 4 December 1955, he explained the art of conducting – how, for example, the first beat in a bar is always down and the last is up. He demonstrated how to vary the beat so as to signal changes in rhythm, moods, and attack, and displaying before the viewers a full score, he interpreted the symbols to them.

The public reacted to this telecast as if the United States was teeming with would-be conductors. Men started practising before mirrors whilst orchestral music flowed from gramophones; and when, shortly after the programme, records of Bernstein's music for fledgling conductors appeared in the shops complete with duplicates of his baton they soon sold out – which is not surprising, for some 75 million people had watched the eight lectures. The latter, too, proved best-sellers, brought out in book form under the title of *The Joy of Music*. The cover carried a photograph depicting Bernstein, in a shocked friend's words, 'like a haggard twentieth-century Prometheus with some sort of vulture tearing at his liver'.

The showman conductor invites adulation, and a surfeit of it, especially from the fair sex, can cause problems. One afternoon Leonard Bernstein had just conducted with students at Tanglewood the final rehearsal of *Rio Grande*, Constant Lambert's work in jazz idiom for chorus and orchestra, when he was introduced to Tallulah Bankhead, who was acting locally in summer stock.

'Darling, I have just gone mad over your back muscles,' she revealed. 'You must come and have dinner with me.'

This was the last thing Bernstein wanted to do, but Tallulah was determined to have her way. Refusing to let him change from his rehearsal clothes of Basque shirt and dungarees lest he escape, she bundled him into her car and set off to Stockbridge for refreshments.

With Tallulah as his companion, Bernstein found that time sped past far more swiftly than he realized, and when at last the prickings of conscience made him look at his watch he saw to his horror that it was 8.00 pm. The concert was due to start in fifteen minutes, with *Rio Grande* second on the programme. Rushed by the siren's chauffeur to his apartment, Bernstein scrambled into formal dress and arrived in the hall just as the opening piece, led by a student conductor, finished. Despite the panic, Bernstein rose to the occasion and his conducting of Lambert's work proved an enormous success.

Bernstein has proved a controversial figure. Oscar Levant has accused him of using music as an accompaniment to his conducting, but George R. Marek considered it wrong to stigmatize Leonard Bernstein's behaviour as out-and-out charlatanism: 'Those falling-locks swoons, that rhythmic pirouetting, the high jumps off the podium, the feline crouching, those Death-and-Transfiguration grimaces, all the mannerisms which prove disturbing to part of the audience and are loved by the old ladies, are these altogether acting?' Marek thought it more probable that they were a necessary part of his technique, employed in all sincerity, for he behaved in exactly the same way during recording sessions when nobody but a few blasé engineers was present.

Whilst the public at large may over-rate conductors skilled in showmanship, the members of the orchestra never do. A player in the Minneapolis Symphony Orchestra once confided to a friend about a conductor: 'Watch him and when he starts making a circular scooping motion with his arms, that will mean, "Keep playing, boys, I'll find my place." '

Herbert Pendergast interviewing Antal Dorati (*Music and Musicians*, June, 1973) quoted Herman Scherchen's contention that mime was one of the conductor's principal tools. Dorati disagreed. He thought that pulling faces while conducting was in poor taste. Jumping into the air and similar clownish behaviour was sometimes caused by inability to communicate with the orchestra. Unfortunately, audiences liked watching podium histrionics. As Claude Debussy wrote in *Monsieur Croche, anti-dilettante*: 'The attraction of the virtuoso for the public is very like that of the circus for the crowd. There is always the hope that something dangerous will happen. Monsieur Ysaye may play the violin with Monsieur Colonne on his shoulders, or Monsieur Pugno may conclude his piece by lifting the piano with his teeth.'

Walter Damrosch wished in his memoirs that it were possible to educate people to listen to music with their ears only and not with their eyes.

A large part of the public are easily gulled and more easily moved if the conductor "dramatizes" the music through his gestures. By the skilful manipulation of his arms and hands, his hips and his hair, he gives the impression that when the 'cellos play a soulful melody, it really drips from his wrists, and when the kettledrums play a dramatic roll, it is really the result of a flash of his eye.

Igor Stravinsky expressed similar views about the choreographic school of conducting in *The New York Review of Books* in 1960. He would not attempt to describe the performance that new conductor X gave in terms of music, except to say that its most winning features were 'a crucifixion, the extended arms motionless and the hands limp in frozen passion, a pelvic thrust co-ordinated with a throwing back of the head, used at climaxes; and a turning of the profile not just toward the first violas but beyond them and out to the audience.' Another innovation had been promised before the show reached Broadway and, according to rumour, it would be 'handstands during inverted counterpoint'. Yet the high point was none of these but 'the after-performance performance'. It began with 'a tableau of moribundity modelled on the Descent from the Cross'. The arms were lifeless, the knees bent, the head (hair artfully disarranged) low, and the whole corpse bathed in perspiration (warm water, one suspected, squirted from hidden atomizers). The first step down from the podium just failed to conceal a totter, but 'in spite of that the miracle-worker somehow manages to reappear forty-six times'. It was a great performance, though, and could be topped as an advertisement only by skywriting. Even a musician could be swept away by it.

Danny Kaye, speaking in 1982 at the Academy Award ceremony, said that to stand before an orchestra and conduct it gave one the greatest feeling of neurotic power in the world; could it be, then, that some dictators of the baton are fit subjects for a psychiatrist's couch?

Impressing the Orchestra

Experienced conductors know that every orchestra has its own characteristics that distinguish it from all others. Their tastes and attitudes vary widely, but orchestral players are shrewd psychologists and 'guest' conductors who try to bluff them do so at their peril. A conductor is most likely to be popular if he has a sense of humour. Sir Thomas Beecham was well aware of this and kept files of jokes he had collected – one to entertain English orchestras, another French, and so on.

The New York Philharmonic has been dubbed the graveyard of conductors. Its members are excellent musicians, but tough and outspoken and proficient at getting their way with the timorous and ineffectual. Even Otto Klemperer, when he was their guest conductor, found himself in trouble through lecturing them too long. 'Aw, Mister Klemps, you talka too much!' bawled Bruno Labate, the oboist, who was barely 5 feet in height but bragged that the small fortune he had banked made him unafraid of any conductor.

Koussevitzky, though not far away at Boston, refused ever to be a guest conductor of the New York Philharmonic because he said they were 'bandits'. Having had a genius such as Toscanini directing them, it is probable that anyone else must have seemed disappointingly tame to them. He once said that every orchestra accustomed to his conducting became demoralized when he left them.

Leonard Bernstein, who proved himself a great conductor with the New York Philharmonic, has expressed succinctly the difficulties facing the young conductor: 'A violinist has a violin and practises it at home, likewise a piccolo or tuba player. But a conductor needs an instrument which is far too expensive to buy, far too large to house, and far too busy to be at his constant disposition. It is a real problem for a young conductor.'

An orchestra is certainly busy. A conductor seeking to impress players with his perspicacity told them: 'One eye has to be on the music, the other on the conductor; one ear is for listening to the rest of the orchestra; and the other for one's own performance.' Hence, if the mouth is operating a mute, only the instrumentalist's nose can afford to be idle.

If a young conductor impresses an orchestra with his talent and trusts them, they will help him in any crisis. André Previn relates how when he first started with the London Symphony Orchestra, the principal horn, Barry Tuckwell, became his friend and gave him some wise advice: 'When you get lost, and you will, everybody does at one time or other, just make some elegant, vague motion and we'll put it all to rights quickly enough. But for God's sake don't lose your nerve and start flagging away at us, then *we'll* get lost and everybody's in trouble.'

In Hollywood, when aged only 20, André Previn conducted an orchestra for the first time, and was faced with a problem. They were all masterly musicians and they were also his friends. How should he treat them? A happy mean between amiability and authority would seem appropriate, but to achieve that might be difficult. Rapping his baton on the desk, he asked the oboe for an A. The players, in prankish mood, smiled to themselves as the oboist hit an A-flat instead.

Previn was taken aback to hear the others scrupulously tuning to it. If he did not correct them, the music would be played in the wrong key. Suddenly his sharp eyes detected slight smiles on the faces of the string section. He considered the score before him until the players stopped. Then, looking up, he once more rapped his baton for attention. Confident now of winning this duel of wits, he told them: 'Everyone transpose a half tone up.' As he gave the first beat, the orchestra was unable to play, for most of the players were shaking with laughter.

Audiences have been known to wonder whether the conductor has so sensitive an ear that he can tell whenever an instrumentalist plays a wrong note. There was a would-be prince of the podium who tried to conceal his inferior musicianship through bluff. He had been given the opportunity of directing a well-established orchestra, and, hoping to impress them, he had deliberately inserted wrong notes into the parts so as to be able to make much of pointing out mistakes.

At the first rehearsal, following a loud chord in the brasses, he threw down his baton and cried: 'The fourth horn played an F sharp. Change it to F natural.' To which the horn-player retorted: 'Maestro, some idiot put in an F sharp, but I know the music – I did play an F natural!'

There are occasions when instrumentalists are themselves at fault, as when, for example, Sir Thomas Beecham chided: 'We cannot expect you to be with us all the time, but perhaps you would be good enough to keep in touch now and again.' Another time, as guest conductor, he was rehearsing an orchestra in which the trombones played extremely loudly, so he paused and said: 'Trombones, would you please give us *forte*.' They came in louder still so, signalling for them to stop, he shook his head. 'No, I'm asking for it to be played *forte*.' The trombones nearly exploded with their further efforts, but Beecham remained dissatisfied. 'I want *forte*,' he told them gently: 'You have been playing consistently *double forte*.'

As a token of their admiration, the members of one orchestra presented Toscanini with an expensive gold watch. There came a time when day after day, to his mounting exasperation, the rehearsals were marred by poor playing. Then he had an inspiration. He bought a cheap watch and, on the next occasion when the orchestra upset him, pulled it out of his pocket with a dramatic gesture, hurled it down on the rostrum and jumped on it with feigned rage. All looked aghast, and for the rest of the rehearsals they played better than ever before.

Another conductor who had a penchant for the *pianissimo* pleaded with the French horns at rehearsal, 'Softer, much softer, softer still, please – please!' At last, the first horn player signalled surreptitiously to his colleagues, when the perfectionist was not looking, and, holding their instruments to their lips, they merely pretended to blow. '*Magnifico!*' exclaimed the maestro. 'Now just a soupçon softer and I shall be satisfied.'

Sometimes, differences of opinion lead to open rebellion. Otto Klemperer in California was rehearsing a Beethoven concerto with

Artur Schnabel as soloist. The pianist was upset by some of the conductor's tempi and, when Klemperer was not looking, tried to signal to the others in the orchestra the tempo he wanted. Unfortunately, he was caught doing this by Klemperer who frowned and, pointing at himself, called, 'Herr Schnabel, the conductor is *here!*' But the pianist was unrepentant and returned, 'Klemperer is there, and I am here – but where is Beethoven?'

Sergei Koussevitzky, however, had the last word, when he stopped a rehearsal to tell a violinist, 'Don't play like an old man!' The retort flashed back: 'You're an old man yourself.' Coolly, Koussevitzky rejoined, 'I know that. But when I conduct like an old man, I will give up the job.'

Some conductors try to impress with abrasive sarcasm. 'This is no sty – you are squealing like pigs!' Leopold Stokowski shouted at his reed players in the heat of a rehearsal; when an old player dared to protest, he fired him.

Sir Malcolm Sargent, tiring of the excuses of a reed player, demanded scornfully, 'What is it this time, your teeth or your reed? If you cannot do better than that, don't come tonight!' The man took Sargent seriously and failed to appear at the concert.

Bruno Walter did not believe in railing at the orchestra. Instead, he drew attention to failings with such sorrow that even the most hardened among them felt ashamed and resolved to do better in future. A violinist is said to have burst into tears when Walter asked in the tones of a tragedian: 'What would Mozart have said if he had heard you play the D on an open string?'

It is the cutting, cruel witticism uttered under stress that is often remembered and repeated most when conductors are discussed. The kindly acts tend to be ignored. Egotist though he was, Leopold Stokowski was also interested, as conductor of the Philadelphia Orchestra, in the welfare of his musicians. One of them held the enviable record of never having missed a performance or a rehearsal. On one occasion his wife was expecting to give birth in a hospital a few minutes' distance away by car. Stokowski instructed the orchestra's librarian to provide him with the score of a work in which the player was needed only at the commencement and at the end, with 500 bars of rest between cues.

When a phone message was received from the hospital that the birth was imminent, Stokowski had the parts distributed. The father-to-be played until he reached the first rest, then, carefully counting to himself, drove to the hospital, saw his tiny son, embraced the mother, and returned to the Academy of Music in time to play bar 501 with his proud record still unbroken.

The flautist Gerald Jackson, writing from personal experience in his book *First Flute*, states that he and his fellows are harassed throughout their working lives by conductors who will attempt to teach them how to play their instruments when the only one they know anything about is the piano. He once challenged a well-known conductor to spot whether he was single- or double-tonguing, and although the man boasted he could always detect the difference, Jackson claims to have foxed him every time.

In Rimsky-Korsakov's *Coq d'or*, there is an exacting clarinet solo. Thomas Russell relates how at a rehearsal the first clarinettist, not being conversant with the work, went badly astray in his part. When the session ended and he was leaving the room, the conductor gaily whistled the passage in question to him, saying: 'There you are, old man, that's how it should go.'

'Oh, yes,' replied the wind player, unimpressed. 'I can *whistle* the damn thing!'

There is an old adage often quoted by members of the orchestra: 'The baton makes no sound.' José Iturbi's variation on this theme went: 'The baton is always in C major.' Garry O'Connor in *The Pursuit of Perfection* sums up the position admirably: 'Good conductors put musicians on their feet, but bad ones give them feet of clay.'

Conducting from Memory

Asked why he never used a score when conducting his orchestra, Dimitri Mitropolous answered, 'Does a lion tamer enter a cage with a book on how to tame a lion?' Many other conductors have spurned having a score before them during performances, and this has resulted in some remarkable feats. Hans von Bülow (who told Richard Strauss 'You must have the score in your head, not your head in the score') directed whole concerts and gave recitals lasting three hours, completely from memory and all without a mistake.

Toscanini prided himself on his ability in this respect. A bassoon player once came and said his instrument was broken and would not sound E flat. The maestro thought for a moment, then replied: 'That's all right. You can rehearse with us. The note of E flat doesn't appear in your music today.'

Mozart was conspicuous among composers who needed no score before them when conducting – and he lived in an era before it was usual even for concerto soloists to play without a score. Once, in Leipzig for a performance of his concerto in C, K.467, he sat down at the keyboard and took out a few notes on a scrap of paper, later explaining to a questioner that the piano part was safely locked up in his desk in Vienna and that he was obliged to take such a precaution 'otherwise people contrive somehow or other to get copies of my scores and print them, while I starve'.

When Wagner was conductor of the London Philharmonic concerts, he rehearsed a Beethoven symphony from memory. As Mendelssohn had always led from a score, the directors thought there must be something radically wrong in Wagner's method and remonstrated with him so strongly that he promised to conduct from the music at the concert. Accordingly, that evening he turned the leaves on his desk from time to time as he conducted the symphony. After the concert, one of the directors came up to him and said: 'Now, Herr Wagner, you must admit that the symphony went much better with the score than without it.' Wagner calmly pointed to the score he had used. It was that of Rossini's *Il barbiere di Siviglia.*

Antal Dorati and Zubin Mehta among others have said they consider eye contact with the players of paramount importance and a score a great hindrance. Leopold Stokowski was one of the first to conduct without a score in the USA. When he first did this, a dear old lady in the audience was overheard saying to her companion: 'Isn't it a shame that that wonderful man can't read a score? Imagine how great he would have been if only he knew how!'

Toscanini, it was alleged, dispensed with scores because he was very near-sighted and did not want to be seen wearing glasses by the public. In 1908 when he conducted for the first time at the Metropolitan Opera, New York, it was reported that he could conduct 60 operas without a score. It was not long before exaggeration had raised the figure to 150 and apocryphal anecdotes about his memory spread.

When, in the early 1930s, Wilhelm Furtwängler and the Vienna Philharmonic held a concert in Berlin, the audience heard that he might depart from his usual rule of not giving an encore. Accordingly, after brilliant renditions of Schubert's Unfinished Symphony and Bruckner's Seventh, the applause went on and on while the maestro and his instrumentalists bowed and bowed.

Suddenly, an attendant appeared carrying an impressive music-stand which he placed on the podium; then, hurrying off, he returned with a heavy score, set this open on the stand and departed. More insistent applause recalled Furtwängler who, up till now, had used no score. Then, concentrating his attention on the sheets before him, he started to conduct Johann Strauss's Emperor Waltz, a composition so familiar to the general public that probably no one in that audience did not know it by heart – except Furtwängler and, being a perfectionist, he was taking no risks.

Among those who have scores in front of them when conducting are Sir Colin Davis, Sir Georg Solti and André Previn, who says that they do not actually look at them very often and adds: 'As for me, even when I do conduct from memory I like having the desk there. I like to be able to reach out and touch it. Without it, I get a curious limbo feeling, like I'm going to pitch over into the violas.'

Sir Charles Hallé once put the case for those who shared his opinion:

There can be no possible advantage in dispensing with the score, a glance at which shows to the conductor the whole instrumentation, and enables him to watch over every detail of the execution, and over the entries of the most secondary instruments. No conductor could write by heart twenty pages of the full score of a symphony, or other work, exactly with the instrumentation of the composer (perhaps the composer himself could not do it); he must therefore remain ignorant, whilst conducting, of what the minor instruments, say the second clarinet, second bassoon, second flute, and many others, have to do – a serious disadvantage. The public, who go into ecstasies over 'conducting by heart' do not know how very easy it is, how much easier, for instance, than playing a concerto or a sonata by heart, at which nobody wonders. Without the score, the conductor has only to be acquainted with the general outline of the composition and its salient features, thus the better the band the easier the task of its chief.

Slimming the Score

On a long journey Sir Thomas Beecham spent two days in a train with a German friend. They amused themselves by discovering how many notes they could remove from Richard Strauss's *Ein Heldenleben* while leaving the music essentially intact. By the time they had finished, fifteen thousand had been struck out. Beecham also felt that Wagner's *Götterdämmerung* could be pruned to advantage. On one occasion, when the orchestra was hard at work on this opera and the Curse motif kept recurring he shouted: 'We've been rehearsing for two hours – and we're still playing the same bloody tune!'

James Agate in *Ego Two* mentioned that, after hearing the last act of *Die Walküre* at Covent Garden, he shocked his fellow critic Peter Page by declaring that 'the old gentleman in the nightgown' needed drastic cutting, and that a competent composer would have covered in ten minutes all that mattered musically. Agate wrote:

I cannot understand people like Ernest Newman who bother about the idiotic plot of *The Ring*. I should like to see all the plot cut out, and the four operas run into one and got through in two hours and three-quarters. What Fafner said to the End-Mutter is not my idea of evidence. This candid confession probably puts me beyond the musical pale. I don't mind.

Actually, Agate need not have feared being so ostracized, for some distinguished musicians have felt that Wagner's masterpieces could be improved by editing. It was in 1908 that, after conducting the Vienna Opera Orchestra for some ten years, Mahler left to take over the same post at the Metropolitan, New York. Previously he had resolutely refused to allow any cuts, whereas in New York he not only adopted the customary ones but even experimented with further excisions. Those he made in *Tristan* were widely resented. The *Musical Courier,* however, approved, claiming that Wagner's operas were too long 'not for the pilgrims at Bayreuth, but for the busy New Yorkers who after working hard all day do not want to be kept in the opera house much more than three hours'. The article pointed out that by careful deletions Anton Seidl used to bring Wagner's works within reasonable lengths without sacrificing any of the best pages. Mr Mahler was following that example, and the *Courier* mentioned approvingly that he had almost promised to reduce the time of Mozart's *Don Giovanni* from three hours and a half to two and three-quarters.

Meanwhile, in Vienna, Mahler's successor, Felix Weingartner, had been denounced by the Austrian critics for conducting *Die Walküre* with considerable cuts. Defending his action, he explained at length in a letter to the *Neue Freie Presse* how, after considering the matter over many years, he had concluded that many parts of *Der Ring des Nibelungen, Tannhäuser* and even the short *Der fliegende Holländer* were too long, not only in actual time but also as regards structure, and so on. He regarded what he had done, therefore, as an artistic duty that greatly enhanced aesthetic pleasure, and he intended to perform similar necessary operations on several other Wagner operas; nor would he yield to any kind of opposition.

All this was to lead to such bad feeling that whilst a rehearsal for *Die Meistersinger* was in progress some heavy scenery mysteriously collapsed, breaking Weingartner's leg, and he eventually left Vienna.

Years earlier, the distinguished Viennese critic Eduard Hanslick had attended the first Bayreuth Festival in 1876 and had written of *Die Walküre*:

The second act is an abyss of boredom. Wotan appears, holds a long conversation with his wife, and then, turning to Brunnhilde, gives an autobiographical lecture covering eight full pages of text. This utterly tuneless, plodding narrative, in a slow tempo, engulfs us like an inconsolable broad sea from which only the meagre crumbs of a few leitmotives come floating towards us out of the orchestra. Scenes like this recall the medieval torture of waking a sleeping prisoner by stabbing him with a needle at every nod. We have heard Wagnerites characterize this second Act as a disaster. It is entirely unnecessary, since with two cuts both episodes could be done away with, painlessly.

Of Wotan's long scene with the dwarf in the first act of *Siegfried*, Hanslick wrote:

Each gives the other three questions, and each answers with the detailed precision of a well-tutored candidate at a school examination. The whole scene, utterly superfluous from the dramatic point of view, is an oppressive bore. The listeners are abandoned to the diversion of hunting hidden leitmotives in the orchestra (where is the cat? where is the bear?). Generally speaking, one can be certain that with the appearance of so much as the point of Wotan's spear, a half-hour of emphatic boredom is in store.

And nearly a hundred years before Hanslick was expressing such feelings, Mozart himself in 1778 admitted in a letter the value of cutting: 'If I have time, I shall rearrange some of my violin concertos and shorten them. In Germany, we rather like length, but after all it is better to be short and good.'

Of course, it is important that such shortening should be attempted only by those with the right musical knowledge. Hector Berlioz in *Les Grotesques de la musique* told a story about a lady singer who called on the well-known music publishers Messrs Brandus and asked to see the latest songs, stressing that she was anxious to obtain something without too many flats in the key signature. The assistant then showed her a romance. 'This is delightful,' he remarked, 'but unfortunately it has four flats.' To which the customer replied: 'Oh, that won't trouble me. When there are more than two, I simply cut them all out!'

A company director unable to attend a performance of Schubert's Unfinished Symphony gave the ticket to a work study consultant, who next day sent him the following criticism:

For considerable periods, the four oboe players had nothing to do. Their number should be reduced, and the work spread more evenly over the whole concert, thus eliminating peaks and troughs of activity. All twelve violins were playing identical notes. This seems unnecessary duplication.

The stuff of this section should be drastically cut: if a large volume of sound is really required, it could be obtained by means of an electronic amplifier.

Much effort was absorbed in the playing of demi-semi-quavers. This seems an excessive refinement. It is recommended that all notes should be rounded up to the nearest semi-quaver. If this were done, it should be possible to use trainees and low-grade operatives more extensively.

No useful purpose is served by repeating with horns a passage which has already been handled by the strings. It is estimated that if all redundant passages were eliminated, the whole concert time of two hours could be reduced to twenty minutes, and there would be no need for an interval.

The work study consultant might have added that as, even after such cuts, there were bound to be times when some members of the orchestra were doing nothing, a further saving could be achieved in future by paying them according to the total number of notes each played.

The impresario Colonel Mapleson in Victorian times tried cutting operas, for reasons of economics, with unfortunate consequences. On Sundays, when there was no third-class service operating between Dublin and England, one had to travel by the expensive mail-boat service and the total fares for a large company might turn a profit of an engagement into a loss. So, finding that a coal-boat taking passengers left at midnight on the Saturday, he reserved all the space needed at a quarter of the cost of travel by mail-boat. He then instructed the conductor to arrange that for the Saturday evening performance one verse only of each number was sung and no encores were given.

On the night itself, however, those in the gallery soon discovered they were not receiving their money's worth. The spectators realized that the signal used by Luigi Arditi for curtailment was two taps on his desk, and the moment these were heard the occupants of the 'gods' turned into howling devils, able to be appeased only when he surrendered to their shouts of: 'Second verse – y'll hav' to go bak, Looeggee – this won't do!'

Mapleson found out later that some of his Italian choristers, who always suffered from seasickness, had incited the gallery to demonstrate in this way, because the Sunday mail-boat took only three-and-a-half hours for the crossing whilst the all-night coal-boat would have subjected them to fourteen hours of misery.

On next returning to Dublin with his flock, the impresario cleverly outwitted the malcontents by staging on the Saturday night a programme of single acts from various operas – and choosing, of course, the shortest. The curtain fell finally at 10.30 pm, allowing adequate time for packing and transferring everything on to the coal-boat, which steamed away at midnight – much to the resentment of those who dreaded long sea journeys.

A similar incident occurred at El Paso in the 1880s, when a touring company presented *Il barbiere di Siviglia* with minor cuts. During the interval, a professional musician in the audience mentioned the omissions to his neighbour. This was overheard by others and within a short while the entire opera house knew about it. General uproar ensued as people climbed on to their seats shouting that they had been cheated and demanding the sheriff.

Sometimes, however, an audience can be fooled. Coenraad von Bos was accompanying Elena Gerhardt in Hugo Wolf's 'Song of the Wind' when she left out two pages in the middle of the *Lied*. Owing to the pianist's skill the audience did not notice this jump, and in fact were so impressed that they called for the song to be repeated. Before Elena began again, Bos whispered to her: 'Won't they be surprised to find it has become longer?'

When it has become the custom to present an opera in a trimmed form, restoration of the discarded passages can have unexpected consequences. In the 1920s, Toscanini revived at La Scala the original version of *Il trovatore*, with '*Di quella pira*' as a duet, 49 bars restored and no high C within earshot.

Later, recalling what then happened, Toscanini said that the audience did not recognize it. 'What's he playing? *Abbasso Toscanini!* That pig doesn't know Verdi!' they objected. He was forced to show people the score, saying: 'Look! It's not me – it's Verdi who wrote this.' They were astounded. They had never looked at it.

Those artists who cater for audiences with little knowledge of music, who frequent concerts chiefly to be entertained, have an easier time. In their case, it is not so much what you play but how you put it over that matters. Liberace once said: 'My whole trick is to keep the tune well out in front. If I play Tchaikovsky, I play his melodies and skip his spiritual struggles. Naturally I condense. I have to know just how many notes my audiences will stand for. If there's time left over, I fill in with a lot of runs up and down the keyboard.'

Conductors about Conductors

It was Verdi who predicted that conductors would become the prima donnas of the future. Certainly some of them have spoken of their rivals in the style of imperious divas. Toscanini never mentioned Sergei Koussevitzky by name, referring to him as 'that Russian boor', while Beecham described Toscanini as 'a glorified bandmaster' and on being told that eye trouble had forced him to memorize scores commented: 'I'm sorry to hear it – indeed a double affliction when you remember for how many years he has been practically tone-deaf.' Later, Otto Klemperer grumbled with assumed despair: 'Because that wretched Italian is myopic, I am expected to learn everything by heart.' And when towards the end of December, 1954, a friend of Klemperer's remarked to him, 'What a number of distinguished conductors have died this year – Clemens Krauss, Wilhelm Furtwängler, Jasha Horenstein. . .' Klemperer interrupted: 'Ja, it's been a good year, hasn't it?'

If a conductor has been knighted, he does not always enjoy hearing that a rival has been similarly honoured. Soon after Malcolm Sargent went to Buckingham Palace to receive the accolade, someone told Sir Thomas Beecham that another conductor played the National Anthem faster than he did. Beecham asked who it was.

'*Sir* Malcolm Sargent,' was the reply.

'I didn't know he'd been knighted,' Sir Thomas said sourly. 'I knew he'd been doctored.'

Beecham was dubbed by Sir John Barbirolli 'the dancing dervish' whilst the former was as disapproving of the latter as he was of all fashionable conductors from abroad. He asked: 'Why do we in England engage at our concerts so many third-rate conductors when we have so many second-rate ones of our own?' And he showed his contempt whenever he met any, as, for example, when emerging from the lift at the Royal Festival Hall he saw facing him an up-and-coming and immaculately groomed young Italian conductor, waiting to ascend. Standing next to him was a shabby, insignificant-looking man. Beecham's companion gushed: 'Oh, Sir Thomas, allow me to introduce Signor Guido Cantelli.'

'How are you? I *am* glad to meet you,' smiled Beecham, shaking hands with the astonished nobody.

Toscanini was just as rude about Sir Thomas himself, labelling him 'an amateur' and 'a buffoon', whilst the Englishman hit back by calling the other 'an old humbug'.

The Italian regarded it as an insult for any other conductor to dare to advise him on how he should conduct. He had a poor opinion of Willem Mendelberg, whom he regarded as far too garrulous, but what really angered him was when Mendelberg came and told him at great length 'the proper German way' to conduct the *Coriolanus* Overture. 'He had got it, he declared very seriously, from a conductor who supposedly had got it straight from Beethoven. "Bah!" I told him. "I got it straight from Beethoven himself – from the score." '

It was enough to make Sir Henry Wood bad-tempered if Sir Thomas, ten years his junior, was mentioned. The latter in 1933 suddenly cancelled a South Coast musical festival engagement, so its organizers appealed to Sir Henry to deputize, offering him a high fee and a generous sum as expenses. But this was insufficient emollient to entirely remove the bruise to Wood's pride. He answered on a postcard, underlining certain words: 'Very well, I will do it for you, but if you ever want me again during my conducting life, don't forget that I am the doyen of British conductors, and as such I think I ought to be consulted about the free dates before everyone else is ... Please excuse card.'

There was also a much-publicized dispute between the two celebrities over who should lead the London Philharmonic, founded by Beecham, when Wood agreed to conduct it at the triennial Sheffield Festival in 1936. After Paul Beard's resignation, Sir Thomas appointed David McCallum as his successor, which made Wood protest that he had never worked with the new leader and must have one accustomed to his ways. There were protracted negotiations and at one stage Beecham offered to let Bernard Andrews lead, then withdrew the proposal in pique because Wood had revealed the matter to the press.

The quarrel now became increasingly acrimonious as the two conductors attacked each other in newspaper interviews. Wood declared that he had 'no intention of bowing the knee' to this 'dictator' – and Beecham fired back that it was the other who wanted to dictate his own terms: 'Suppose Toscanini and myself were invited to conduct at, say, Munich, and then said: "Oh yes, I should be delighted, but I must have my own leader. He is a very capable and good fellow." The authorities would very properly reply: "Very well, stay away." ' He thought Wood's attitude 'fantastic'. Unwisely, the latter then told a reporter that, having been a professional conductor longer than anyone else, he must know best how to maintain standards in performance.

This drew a broadside from Beecham: 'Sir Henry refers to his forty-two years' experience as a concert conductor and is polite enough to suggest that, compared with this, my own experience is negligible. I can only reply that for the past thirty-four years I have been before the public not only as a conductor of concerts but also of opera, the latter branch being an infinitely more arduous medium.' This was an oblique thrust at Wood's inexperience in that respect. 'So far as orchestras are concerned,' Beecham went on, 'I have been privileged to found no fewer than four new ones in this country. The suggestion of Sir Henry's that I am not competent to express an opinion in this matter passes from the zone of the fantastic to the less agreeable one of the impertinent. When I described his attitude as fantastic, I did so because I was certain that such an attitude would be taken up by no other conductor in the world.'

The bickering continued for a while until Wood accepted defeat, and the Festival organizers issued a face-saving statement to the effect that so as not to disappoint music-lovers Sir Henry Wood would conduct after all and allow David McCallum to lead.

Sir Malcolm Sargent, who scrupulously avoided ever squabbling in public with Beecham, said of him to Charles Reid that he got what he wanted by 'devilish brilliance', and that at times he was 'almost cheeky', having 'a Svengali-like assurance'; while Sir Hamilton Harty, asked why he did nothing to further opera in Manchester, shrugged and quipped: 'Opera in the provinces is dying of T.B.'

Sir Thomas omitted to mention in his public rejoinder to Sir Henry Wood that during his long career he had conducted the ballet as well as concerts and opera. Here, too, he could not resist jesting at another's expense. In 1934 when the Ballets Russes held a season at Covent Garden he shared the conducting of performances with Antal Dorati, who one morning began the rehearsals with Beecham taking over half-way. In those days, Dorati used extremely long batons because he thought they made him look more elegant in action. On leaving the podium he went to sit in the front stalls, but forgot to remove his baton from the stand. He watched Sir Thomas greet the orchestra, then stare thoughtfully at the outsize stick for a moment or so before picking it up and waving it to and fro at arm's length. He paused and, looking round, remarked: 'Mr Dorati, I didn't know you were a fisherman.'

Rivalry over rates of pay has also caused trouble between conductors. Toscanini once agreed to take part in an important festival of Verdi's music. A musician of lesser distinction who envied the maestro's success was invited to conduct as well, but would not accept the engagement unless he was paid one lira more than Toscanini. To this the organizers agreed. Then the other learnt to his dismay that Toscanini, on account of his admiration for Verdi, had refused payment of any kind.

What is the worst insult one can pay to a conductor? In 1859, the Royal Italian Opera Company held a season at the Theatre Royal, Drury Lane, and two conductors, Luigi Arditi and Sir Julius Benedict, were engaged. Both had, as a reporter put it, 'glorious bald knobs'. One evening before a grand combined performance, Colonel Mapleson, the impresario, happened to enter the prima donna's dressing-room, and there stood Sir Julius before the mirror using her brush and comb to try to re-arrange his scanty locks so as to cover as much as possible of his denuded cranium.

'What are you doing?' enquired Mapleson.

'Nothing in particular, only I don't want to be mistaken for Arditi.'

Soon after Sir Julius had left, Arditi appeared and, going to the dressing-table, carefully camouflaged his bald spot, saying in his curious falsetto, 'I don't want to be mistaken for Benedict.'

Drowning the Singers

Opera singers mostly believe that the time for conductors to show off their talent is during the overture, and that for the rest of the performance they should accompany the singers. Maurice Grau, who managed the new Metropolitan Opera, New York, after the fire of 1892 and who was responsible for Melba's American début there, ran it profitably by paying the stars high fees and spending little on all else, including conductors – on the grounds that 'nobody ever paid a nickel to see a man's back'.

Gerald Moore, with long experience as a concert accompanist, stressed in his *Farewell Recital*:

As I have written elsewhere, the great burden of responsibility falls on the singer; it is he who *presents* the song, who marries the words with the music . . . and I have never lost sight of this vital fact. Conductors *qua* conductors will have none of this: listening to them accompanying a singer on the pianoforte I have sometimes wondered if they so much as listen to the voice for they will romp and slap about like babies in the bathtub.

Blanche Marchesi, writing in the early 1920s, claimed that in England at orchestral rehearsals she was aware of barely disguised contempt on the faces of members of the orchestra, and that throughout her career it had seemed to her that they considered singers as beings who learnt words and music like parrots, who always wanted to finish with a top note so as to gain an ovation, and who did not at all care if what they did was artistic or not. Typical of the attitude to which she refers is the quip of the musician who, asked whether a soprano could hit E above top C, said: 'Only when a newspaper reports her real age.'

Some 150 years previously, Dr Burney, describing his travels in Italy, had related how the celebrated *castrato* Farinelli, soon after making his début in opera, at the age of fifteen, engaged in a nightly musical duel with a renowned trumpet player while singing in Rome.

This at first seemed amicable and merely sportive, till the audience began to interest themselves in the contest and to take different sides. After severally swelling a note in which each manifested the power of his lungs and tried to rival the other in brilliancy and force, they had both a swell and shake together, by thirds, which was continued so long, while the audience eagerly awaited the event, that both seemed exhausted; and in fact the trumpeter, wholly spent, gave it up . . . when Farinelli, with a smile on his countenance, showing he had only been sporting with him all that time, broke out all at once in the same breath, with fresh vigour . . . and was at last silenced only by the acclamations of the audience.

Hans Richter, when he became conductor of the Hallé, declared: 'If the expenses are too big, let us cut out the stars. We do not need them. We are stars ourselves. People do not come to hear singers – they come to hear the orchestra.' And when vocal numbers were required he engaged the cheapest available new talent, with the result that box-office receipts fell.

Toscanini, though not holding so extreme a view, believed that the orchestra was just as important as the vocalists, which did not lead to popularity with the latter. Chaliapin described him as 'the damnedest lump of macaroni to swallow', but admitted he was the only conductor who scared him and made him feel like a pupil. Singers certainly feared Toscanini but knew that, if lashed with his anger, they could blame themselves for daring to sustain notes or indulge in *rubati* or *rallentandi*.

In a battle between the singer and the conductor, supported by his heavy artillery, the latter is bound to win. A British exception might have been Dame Clara Butt, whose voice, according to Beecham, could on a clear day be heard in Paris. Before directing *Elektra* for the first time at Covent Garden, he told the orchestra: 'The singers think they're going to be heard, and I'm going to make jolly well certain that they are not.'

Some said that Sir Thomas was following the example of the opera's composer, Richard Strauss. Legend has it that at the rehearsals before the Dresden première, when the conductor, concerned for the singers, reduced the orchestral sound, Strauss protested: 'But, my dear Schuck, I insist you make them play louder – I can still hear the voice of Frau Heink!'

What really happened was that Strauss, nagging at Ernst von Schuck in an attempt to make him liven up the orchestra, so exasperated him that when the first night arrived Schuck conducted with such fury that Ernestine Schumann-Heink's famed big robust voice was drowned and, finding the ordeal of singing Klytemnestra too severe, she relinquished the role after only one performance.

But it would be wrong to give the impression that conductors are usually on a collision course with vocalists. Norman K. Miller, administrator of the Royal Philharmonic Orchestra for ten years from 1948, recalls Sir Thomas Beecham conducting a performance of *The Bohemian Girl*, by Balfe, during the Festival of Britain. A tenor playing a leading role told Beecham that often, when he looked at his conductor, the expression on the man's face would constrict his throat and undermine his assurance, but when he looked at Sir Thomas's face he saw an expression which said to him that this was to be one of the loveliest sounds Sir Thomas had heard and, as a result, the tenor found himself producing a voice he scarcely knew he owned.

Bruno Walter was always on the best of terms with singers. Lotte Lehmann said of him: 'When he accompanies me, I have a feeling of the utmost well-being and security. The end of his baton is like a cradle in which he rocks me.'

There is another weapon which a conductor can employ, if he is so minded, in his battles with singers – lighting. When Karajan conducted *Die Walküre* at the Metropolitan in December, 1967, with Birgit Nilsson as Brünnhilde, he made her sing in nearly total darkness. Even when she came on to the stage wearing a miner's helmet with a lantern attached, she failed to make him change his mind.

After that she would not appear under Karajan's baton. The *New York Times* reported her as saying:

I still don't think he himself knows how wrong he is in his productions. . . . When he makes all these light rehearsals, or dark rehearsals, he doesn't count on the fact that the orchestra pit is not lit. When the performance comes, he brings the pit up higher – you can see him from the knees up and he has a spotlight on him, of course.

The public gets all the light from the orchestra pit in their eyes. And the stage remains dark. It's insane, and nobody dares to tell him because they're afraid of him. This is the way Karajan feels he is great – that he has the power and nobody is worth anything around him.

*'Patience, patience, Enrico —
with any luck they'll start
shedding the load just as she
reaches top E.'*

It's the Music that Matters

A player in the Hallé orchestra had an affair with a young soprano.
It went on for some time before a mischief-maker informed his
wife. There was a stormy scene, ending with her rushing off and
bursting into Sir John Barbirolli's sanctum in the Free Trade Hall
during a concert interval.

'What can I do for you?' the conductor asked.

'It's my husband,' she sobbed. 'He's carrying on with this singer,
and I don't know what to do.'

'My dear,' replied Barbirolli, 'you know there's nothing to worry
about. He's playing better than ever.'

'It's Ravel's "Concerto for the Left Hand"'

Women in the Orchestra

Baldassare Castiglione in his book *The Courtier* (1528) asked his readers to try to picture in their mind's eye a woman beating a tabor or drum, blowing a flute or trumpet, or playing any like instrument. It would be a repellent sight 'because the boisterousness of them doth ... take away that sweet mildness which should accompany every deed a woman does'.

Much earlier, about 190 BC, in the *Book of Wisdom*, Ben Sira had warned men: 'Consort not with a female musician lest thou be taken in by her snares.' But some might argue that such advice is valid when a son of Adam associates with any Eve. Less misogynic is the Spanish proverb: 'To use a woman or a guitar, one must know how to tune them.'

'The trouble with women in an orchestra,' Sir Thomas Beecham has said, 'is that if they are attractive it will upset my players, and if they are not it will upset me.' Later, insisting that he was very fond of the fair sex, he regretted that when there *were* women in an orchestra, they were often plain and always looked worse when they were blowing, which put him off – 'while if they *are* good-looking, it puts me off a damned sight more'.

Zubin Mehta, interviewed by the *New York Times*, said he disapproved of women being in orchestras he conducted: 'They become men. Men treat them as equals. They even change their pants in front of them. I think it's terrible.' But Sir Malcolm Sargent was all in favour of women following his baton, declaring: 'The man who is not thrilled to the bone by the sight of a woman playing the flute, blowing a clarinet or struggling with the intricacies of a trombone is no man.'

Sir Henry Wood was actually the first English conductor to

employ women in a symphony orchestra, which he did so that they could take the places of men called up in the First World War. Sidonie Goossens relates how, when she joined his orchestra at the Queen's Hall in the early 1920s, she found he did not like women cellists because they showed too much leg, at a time when shorter skirts and flesh-coloured stockings were becoming fashionable. Miss Goossens continues: 'Lady Wood, the old Lady Wood, came to us, the harpists, and asked us to tell the ladies to wear gunmetal-coloured stockings because Sir Henry was too distracted. His eyes kept going down to those light-coloured legs.'

Sir Thomas Beecham did not approve of women cellists, but in his case it was for a different reason. Pausing during a rehearsal, he told one to stand up, then said, 'You have between your legs the most sensitive instrument known to man, and all you can do is to sit there and scratch it.'

And as for women conductors, according to Schonberg, they have one advantage over men: 'A musician knows when the upbeat begins because that is when the slip starts to show.'

'Call yourselves gentlemen…'

Flying Saucers

Life in the orchestra pit can be hazardous when badly aimed bouquets – and sometimes less pleasant missiles – intended for the singers on the stage, fall short of the target. Opera glasses, handbags, coffee cups and saucers, too, perched precariously on the ledges of boxes, are liable to be sent flying down when the occupants, carried away by the vocal fireworks, lean over or jump heedlessly when applauding. Then there are the properties used during the course of the opera, such as crockery and glassware which can cause blood to flow when striking a bald cranium – and, of course, one must not forget the dust from too vigorous dancing and other frolicking, and the unpleasant experience of singers salivating over the unfortunate instrumentalists.

For example, one of the last of the pea-soup fogs that used to blot out London occurred in the early 1950s when Inia Te Wiata was singing Colline in *La Bohème* at Covent Garden. It even drifted into the auditorium and made it difficult for the cast to see the conductor. Wiata and Geraint Evans had to rush about the stage in a mock fight with poker and coal-shovel, culminating with their jumping on to a bed and having a pillow fight. They became somewhat over boisterous and the poker burst a pillow, the feathers floating down into the pit, getting stuck in the instruments and making the players sneeze, cough and splutter.

Practical Jokes

Some musicians enjoy playing practical jokes. The singer addicted most to this form of fun was Caruso. The majestic Melba put up with his foolery, but was furious when once stagehands played a trick on her. At Covent Garden, her dictatorial ways antagonized them. Being an Australian, she found wattle gum soothed her throat; before singing she would deposit the piece she had been chewing on a glass ledge in the wings and pop it back again on leaving the scene. One evening after the final curtain of *La Bohème*, she picked up what ought to have been the gum, then immediately spat the stuff out again in disgust. Someone had substituted a quid of strong shag.

Even Toscanini was not above playing practical jokes. In New York, he bought from a Times Square store some toy mice, which he would wind up and let loose on the stage to terrify nervous sopranos; at his parties he would serve the guests with drinks in glasses perforated with tiny holes, through which the liquor would slowly trickle.

It is perhaps only natural that instrumentalists, confined in the orchestra pit, should be tempted into relaxing horseplay on occasion. Even women have done this, such as the bassoonist who, one afternoon after the players had celebrated the conductor's birthday, slipped back ahead of the others and fitted the base of a rubber glove over the mouth of her bassoon, then pushed the fingers inside. When the rehearsal was resumed, they remained there until she played a low B flat which shut every hole.

'Good God, I shouldn't have drunk so much!' thought the conductor, nearly dropping his baton, as he saw a hand gradually emerge from the bassoon's mouth.

If players are to indulge in such *joie de vivre*, they should be
certain that their conductor has a sense of humour. Holding his
baton rather finically between his fingers, Fritz Reiner used to
make such tiny movements with it that a short-sighted player at the
back of the orchestra brought a brass telescope to a rehearsal, set it
up and peered through it at the podium. What he saw was Reiner
glaring at him, as he shouted: 'You're sacked!'

Another instance where larking led to trouble was when, during
the 1924–5 season at La Scala, Adriano Lualdi's opera *Il diavolo
nel campanile* had its première at La Scala, and the first rehearsals
were directed by Toscanini's staff conductor, Vittorio Gui. There
was a place in the score where the musicians were instructed to
play whatever they pleased. Such licence for free improvisation
led to some clowns in the orchestra making vulgar oral and
instrumental noises and Gui let them have their fun. But when,
despite his repeated warnings, they did this to excess at the dress
rehearsal, then, as Enrico Minelli, one of the players, later related:
'He literally put his foot down, and the cloud of dust that went up
from the podium after he had angrily stamped his feet caused
further noises – of protest, this time – from the orchestra.'

Beside himself, Gui raced away to tell Toscanini all about it,
Minelli continues:

The maestro suddenly like an avalanche came down the steps leading into
our basement waiting-room, screaming as I had never heard him scream
before. Looking like a Fury, he seized one side of a very heavy table that
was in the middle of the room, shook it and made it dance, while
continuing to scream and dare us to fight him. . . . My colleagues, pressed
against the walls, their faces livid, tried to escape. One managed to reach
the W.C. and a few the next room. . . . The principal double-bass, poor
fellow, had the nerve to defend himself saying he was in no way guilty.
Toscanini, in his wrath, attacked him, too, with every insult in his
vocabulary, then still challenging us to risk fighting him, raving and
threatening, he left nursing his wrist which he had injured struggling with
the table. We were all shaking with fear.

Then, next morning, Toscanini returned. The electric lights had
fused. Someone managed to find a candle and light it. Whilst
others struck matches, Toscanini murmured a greeting. 'Everyone
present was a bit embarrassed,' Minelli recalled. 'It was at this

point that our old, half-crazy bass clarinet player – the one who lived in an attic with a chicken – spoke the famous phrase about "the sun and the candles" in a clear allusion, after which the maestro muttered "Imbecile!" in a half-gruff tone, and left. Peace had been made.'

Luigi Arditi, the conductor, tells in his memoirs how Mme Titiens, the nineteenth-century prima donna, always insisted when touring in America on having a hotel suite with a room where she could put out the costumes for every character in her repertoire. A member of the orchestra given to pranks gained admittance to this garde-robe whilst she was out and busied himself stuffing all the dresses, fixing bewigged false heads on to the shoulders, then seated the dozen human-looking figures so produced on chairs around the dimly-lit room. That evening, Titiens went into the room to fetch a costume. A moment later, frightened out of her wits, she rushed downstairs shrieking for the manager and told him when he appeared that either she had gone mad or the ghosts of Norma and other long-dead characters had come to haunt her.

The practical jokes of today's free and easy society would have shocked Mme Titiens' generation. Robert Merrill, the American tenor, wrote in his autobiography, *Between the Acts*: 'A bosom is one of woman's crowning glories, but on stage it can be a pain in the neck.' He continues that in a production of Verdi's *La forza del destino* at the old Metropolitan Eileen Farrell, 'one of the most relaxed and uninhibited of sopranos', played his sister. During dress rehearsals, as he lay dying, she sang her heartbreaking aria 'bending over me and smothering me with her magnificent poitrine'. He whispered: 'Got a cookie with the milk?' which made her swallow 'a few notes in that round'.

At the evening performance, Eileen Farrell approached him singing her lament and 'swinging her treasure chest'. Then, murmuring 'Okay, that's enough', she stuffed with her upstage hand a 'gooey' cookie into his mouth.

Orchestras in the 'Good' Old Days

The Leipzig Gewandhaus is the oldest concert organization in the world. Next to be founded was the Royal Philharmonic Society, in 1813, when there was no permanent orchestra in London sufficiently competent to perform symphonic works. The closest in capability was that of the Concert of Ancient Music, instituted in 1776, the constitution of which allowed only music composed more than twenty years previously to be performed.

Nearly a hundred years later, this body remained as rigidly conservative in its policy. In 1872, the Rev. J.E. Cox commented in his *Musical Recollections of the Last Half Century*:

The Ancient Concerts were dry-as-dust affairs, made up from year to year with odds and ends from old, and not infrequently from comparatively modern, masters, slovenly performed and carelessly conducted. . . . An outsider was able now and then to gain admission, but only to be wearied to death with the unceasing round of dull formality which marked the performances, which were directed in turns by an archbishop, dukes (royal and otherwise), lords, and a member or two of the commonalty who had blue blood in their veins.

Soon after his arrival in New York in September, 1848, Max Maretzek, the opera manager from Paris, went to a performance of *Il barbiere di Siviglia* in the new Astor Place Opera House, and wrote later at length to Hector Berlioz describing the experience:

The orchestra had a leader, Signor Lietti, who did not apparently consider it necessary to indicate the movement by beating the time. On the contrary, he was occupied in playing the first violin part, fully unconscious of the other instruments. But I wrong him. In order to guide them, he was

68

possessed with the monomania of playing more loudly and vigorously upon his fiddle than any of his subordinates. He trampled on the floor as though he had been determined to work a path through the deal planking, and made a series of the most grotesque faces with his nose, mouth and eyes. If you have ever seen a Nuremberg nut-cracker in full operation, you will enter into my feelings as my eyes were riveted on what appeared to me the most extraordinary mechanism of this individual.

In the meantime, the other fiddlers being unwilling to allow Signor Lietti's violin a greater preponderance of sound, exerted themselves with a purely musical ferocity which you have never seen equalled. I have (although it must be owned, not often) upon this side of the Atlantic. It was necessary, however, that Lietti should be heard by the wind-instruments. He therefore began to *scrape* his fiddle. For a moment I actually imagined he had succeeded. But until then, I had not been aware that "diabolical possession" had long survived the time of the Apostles. It has, my dear Berlioz, and the players upon stringed instruments are indisputably subject to it.

After the first eighty bars of the allegro movement, you would, had you been there, upon shutting your eyes have undoubtedly believed that you were surrounded by a series of saw-mills in vigorous operation. Under such circumstances, the leader could not, of course, be heard. They soon came out of time (how could they keep it?) and confusion ensued. Everybody felt himself individually called upon to restore order. A squeak from the *piccolo* would be heard, followed by a loud squall from all the wind-instruments, trying to indicate a place for reunion. Then came a broadside from the trombones and horns, to restrain the already too advanced violins. It was in vain. The screech from the first trumpet was of no use. Even the kettledrum player, who began to beat the right time *fortissimo* on his instrument, was totally unable to stay the confusion. Each went his own way, and made his own speed. Rossini's delicate overture was treated by them, as history tells us some unfortunate criminals were treated in the Middle Ages. These were tied by arm and leg to the hindquarters of four wild horses, which were then driven by the scourge in different directions.

At last, struggling and worn out, one after the other, some few completely distressed, and Signor Lietti by no means first in, they terminated the overture. The audience bestowed upon them a round of applause, and the leader demonstrated by three low bows, his intense satisfaction both with himself and the public.

Signor Lietti and many of his instrumentalists came from Italy, where the standards of playing were hardly any better. A quarter of a century earlier George Sievers, a German scholar residing in Italy, wrote criticizing the lack of technical skill of orchestras in opera houses there:

Passages that are not at all difficult are mangled; indeed, the player often breaks down completely. . . . Everybody fiddles and blows with all his might and main! . . . They play everything at the inspiration of the moment – nothing is thought through . . . Since there are no public concerts, they have no experience in performing so-called symphonies . . . Even more noticeable is the negligence and lack of enthusiasm – it is a case of every man for himself. They tune their instruments while the singer is singing a bravura passage, talk while they are playing, put their instruments down when they feel like resting or scratching their heads. . . .

When the violinist leader gives the sign to begin, he strikes the brass candleholder of his desk several times with all his might, then immediately draws his bow for the first stroke of the work, quite unconscious whether all the rest, or only a few, or in fact anybody at all, begins with him at the same time. These heartrending blows on the candleholder are repeated many times before each number, first by the cembalist, who accompanies the simple recitative on the piano, and later by the first violin. During the recitatives the other players creep under the seats of the orchestra to chat with one another, take a pinch of snuff, or even play a practical joke on one of their colleagues.

When the leader bangs on the candleholder, they rush out in all directions, two-thirds of them usually too late because in their haste one has knocked over a stand, another a candleholder, another the music, or has stepped on a colleague's corn and stops to argue with him. In Paris, the players are not allowed to leave their seats except in the utmost necessity. The Italian musicians, who take good care of their heads, all wear red caps which make them look like the French revolutionaries of 1790.

Berlioz, in his account of his travels in Italy, had similar complaints to make. He was appalled by 'the wretched blowing and scraping, as indifferent to what is being shouted on the stage as to what is being buzzed in the boxes and parterre, and possessed of but one thought – that of earning their supper'.

It was little better in Vienna and parts of Germany. Vincent Novello in his diary for 1829 described a visit to a performance of *Don Giovanni* at the Kärtnerthor in Vienna. He had the same fault to find with the orchestra there as with almost every one that he had heard. They played so boisterously that the singers were obliged to bawl in self-defence in order to be heard. However, the orchestra at Mannheim he had found no better. The overture to Auber's *La Muette de Portici* had begun with a discord and 'the tappage occasioned by the furious blowing of the wind instruments and the violent drumming was hideously noisy'. When the first act's finale was reached: 'The crowing, shouting, bawling, and the furious crashing of the orchestra was enough to split our ears – it was absolutely frightful.' As for the finale of the fourth act, it consisted 'of more trumpeting, drumming, bursting of trombones and smashing of cymbals'.

In contrast H.F. Chorley, the great English music critic, visiting Paris nine years later, wrote that 'the *soi-disant* most perfect orchestra in Europe' was that of the Conservatoire there. He found the playing of the wind instruments beyond all praise. 'No unfortunate flute there chirps half a note before its time – no plethoric bassoon drops one of its thick Satyr-like tones in the midst of a pause – no horn totters on the edge of coarse and mail-coach falseness when the tug of difficulty comes!'

But in the French provinces, according to the historian Castil-Blaze, orchestras were poor. He attended a performance of one opera where no parts were provided: the conductor-violinist and the bass-player used the score, and a few wind players relied on their memories or followed the voices. Elsewhere, he saw two clarinettists playing the same solo together, as their amour-propre would not allow either to be relegated to the second part. He came across an orchestra without any wind players, because they were in dispute with the string players; as a result, for a whole month operas were performed with only string accompaniment. Audiences were by then clamouring for flutes, horns and clarinets, so the string players were given a long holiday, and for quite a time the music for all operas was played only by bassoons, clarinets, horns and trombones.

'The double-bass player has just died – the first horn and the flute have enlisted!' a delighted opera director told Castil-Blaze. 'Now I can save three salaries!' When it was pointed out to him that there must be a first horn, he replied: 'Of course, the second can play the part.' When another protested that a double-bass was absolutely necessary, the retort came: 'Well, haven't we got a cellist? And as for the flautist, the clarinet is there to take his place.

One more or less, the public will be quite satisfied – it isn't so exacting.'

In England, an anonymous writer in the *Musical World* for 28 February 1852 criticized the Philharmonic orchestra's oboes for never being in tune and the stumbling horns for not knowing their parts, and described the trombones as 'ear-splitting Bartlemy-Fair bulls of Bashan'. Earlier, in 1833, the French composer Adolphe Adam complained that the players at Covent Garden were at their worst on Saturday nights, after being paid, because they would immediately get drunk. He attended a performance on such a night and described the astonishing noises the instrumentalists made when they began to play the overture. The oboe went 'COUAK', followed by an extraordinary 'COUAK' from the clarinet. The bassoon let out a succession of stunning snores. The flute made louder and louder 'TURLUTUTUS' whilst another player slipped the bell of his trumpet into the pocket of the man next to him and blew through the clothing – and the bass drum banged 'RUMPUTTITUM' in a frenzy. Meanwhile, the conductor and the singers went on as though all this was quite normal.

Even by the last decade of the nineteenth century, playing in some places gave cause for criticism. Adby Williams in the *Musical Times* for October, 1895, wrote, after attending a performance of *Il barbiere* in Pisa: 'The conductor had to beat time on his desk so often in order to keep his forces together, that he had a small sheet of copper fastened on it to save wearing it out.'

Part of the trouble was that instrumentalists were shamefully ill-paid and worked under miserable conditions. All except cellists in those 'good' old days had to stand when playing. It was not until 1905 that the orchestra at the renowned Leipzig Gewandhaus was allowed to sit. In contrast, it was the tradition for opera conductors to sit both at rehearsals and at performances. A photograph taken as late as 1910 shows Toscanini seated whilst rehearsing the orchestra at the Metropolitan.

But some will argue that standards have not improved in comparison with all periods in the past. Sir Henry Wood in his private papers for 1942 maintained that discipline was not what it had been at the start of his career: 'It is nothing now for a wind player to miss a cue, because he is reading his daily paper or smoking a cigarette, head well down, hidden as he thinks behind his desk. . . . A lady player put her violin on her lap and held a running conversation with a gentleman near by.'

During a performance of Tchaikovsky's Fifth Symphony, to Sir Henry's amazement, a horn player turned and stuck the bowl of his instrument on his neighbour's head. 'I am very sorry – but he was playing so badly,' he apologized in the interval to Wood.

An Upstage Band

It seems incredible today that as late as just before the First World War there were still some who regarded actors and actresses as wandering vagabonds. When touring in 1913 with his company, Sir Thomas Beecham visited an English provincial town and prepared to present *Die Meistersinger*. For the second scene of the final act, requiring a stage orchestra of some dozen players, he engaged the local theatre's band. In *A Mingled Chime*, he relates that at the first rehearsal when the time came for them to play, they remained in the wings. He signalled to them to go up on to the little platform of the set, but they ignored him.

Assuming that the band's behaviour might be due to discontent with their rates of pay, he asked their leader to join him in the auditorium and tactfully enquired if that were the case. But the man interrupted him and said firmly: 'It's not the brass, mister, we've no complaint about that. But me and some of my mates have played in this theatre for sixteen years, and we are all respectable men. None of us have ever been in any sort of trouble, and we are not going to be bloomin' actors for you or anybody else.'

Failing to persuade the band to change their minds, Beecham was forced to 'the expedient of dressing up a body of supers, who pretended to blow into dummy instruments while the real players remained hidden from view behind the scenes!'

Tuning Up

Charles Dickens in *A Christmas Carol* described a fiddler's tuning up as sounding 'like fifty stomach-aches'. Francis Bacon nearly two and a half centuries earlier pointed out in *The Advancement of Learning* 'that noise or sound which musicians make while they are tuning their instruments is nothing pleasant to hear, but yet is a cause why the music is sweeter afterwards'.

In the eighteenth century out-of-tune playing by musicians was common and mostly unavoidable. Audiences were resigned to it, grumbling only when the dissonances became absolutely unbearable. The standard of playing by orchestras in those days was so poor that it would not be tolerated nowadays.

Bernard Shore in *The Orchestra Speaks* describes how, when Willem Mendelberg became conductor of the BBC orchestra, he prefaced the first rehearsal with an interminable discourse on his wonderful experiences all over the world conducting every noteworthy orchestra. At last, he said: 'Zo, you see there is nothing I don't know!' and with a benign 'God help you!' he concluded, 'Now give me the A, Mr Oboe.'

The tuning that followed was a show in itself, beginning with the violins taking the A from the oboe, then the violas, cellos and basses, followed by the flutes and ending with the tuba. Only when the whole orchestra had the A were the strings permitted to tune their other strings. The oboe had to act like a high priest, being obliged to stand facing the department concerned for the benefit of those at a distance, while Mendelberg, squatting on the podium, would detect instantly the smallest variation in pitch. In the end he complained:

Eet has taken twenty-five minutes to tune – it should take two minutes!
Der rehearsal, it begin wid tuning – eet ees no good, unless you are in tune!
. . . It ees difficult now for musicians – fifty years ago it did not matter so
much perhaps; but now it is necessary to haf full haus, and if you play not
in tune, vell? Der haus, eet will be empty! Der feerst oboe, feerst clarinet
moost help der colleagues, like a mutter her children; and, you, Mr Oboe,
moost make ze face, if someone play bad A! You much vatch, like der cat
der mouse. Zere – dat leetle double bass, you hear heem behind zere?

We learn from Bernard Shore, who then played in the BBC
orchestra, that Mendelberg inspired them to do their utmost, with
the result that tuning eventually came down to five or six minutes.

Shore also says that Sir Henry Wood had one of the finest ears
and was keen to investigate different methods of tuning. For years,
members of the orchestra, with the exception of the percussion
players, were ordered to parade in the artists' room before concerts
to take the two As, one wind, one strings, from a home-made
barrel-organ churned by a gloomy-looking man. For half an hour,
players would file past tuning their instruments while an alert and
cheerful Sir Henry, seated in an armchair, gave his verdict of 'Too
sharp!' or 'Too flat!'

Harold Schonberg states that in the early days of the Queen's
Hall orchestra, Sir Henry had a tuning machine built; this was a
silver harmonium with a reed blown by a bellows in a small wind
chest tuned at exactly 435.5 vibrations per second at 59°F and he
made every instrumentalist use it to tune up.

According to Bernard Shore, tuning among the basses – or
doghouses, as they are sometimes known – is always a little
suggestive of the stables, while no other instrumentalists make
such a cacophony when tuning than the cellists. He suggests that
'the effect of the continual tuning of the cello is possibly the reason
for the pensiveness of their next-of-kin'.

There is a tale about a conductor who during a rehearsal became
increasingly irritated by some of the cellos sounding out of tune.
Eventually, he ordered them all to queue outside his room so that
he could inspect their instruments in turn and tune them. The
players, however, fooled him. As each emerged, he handed his
instrument to the next in line with the result that the conductor kept

on retuning the same cello. When the inspection was over, the rehearsal was resumed and the conductor expressed nothing but satisfaction with the sound of the cellos for the rest of the session.

'That's done it! — you've hit on the mating call of the yellow-nosed hornet.'

Fiddle

Ambrose Bierce in his *Devil's Dictionary* cynically defined a fiddle as 'an instrument to tickle human ears by friction of a horse's tail on the entrails of a cat', whilst Jeremy Collier in *An Essay on Musick* wondered: 'What can be more strange than that the rubbing of a little Hair and Cat-gut together make such a mighty alteration in a Man that sits at a distance?'

The Hungarian gypsies, prisoners of the British Army in Italy, who had listened to Walter Starkie give a violin recital in January, 1919, came to him afterwards to ask for packing-cases, out of which they made fiddles and bows. In his book *Raggle-Taggle* he wrote: 'They were grotesque objects, these raw-white packing case fiddles and they had only a string here and there, but they worked their spell when throbbing under the devilish fingers of the gypsies. So contagious was their music that the stolid British soldiers . . . began to dance like dervishes.'

One of the gypsies told a story popular in Transylvania about a village girl who had failed to make a young farmer return her love. The Devil appeared and promised to provide her with a magic instrument which would ensnare the youth, but first she had to give the fiend her father, mother and four brothers, which she did. In return, the Devil formed a case out of the father's body, a bow out of the mother's white hair, and strings out of the four brothers. Then, handing the fiddle to the girl, he bade her play it in her loved one's ear.

Of course, the farmer fell for the girl's playing and the Devil, as the price for his services, took them off with him to Hell. As for the violin, a ragged gypsy found it. 'And he, stranger,' the prisoner told Starkie, 'is playing it yet throughout the world, and because it is the Devil's instrument men and women go daft when they hear it, and the Gypsy alone knows its secret.'

There is a proverb that says you can make a peasant drunk on a glass of water and a gypsy fiddle. As he travelled later through Transylvania, Starkie says that he certainly found it true of the peasants there. Music was an essential vent for their feelings. Once, in a café, he looked closely at some of these fiddles. They were a sorry sight, having suffered the extremes of one day being roasted in the sun and another of being soaked in a cloud-burst, and furthermore they were carried about in threadbare bags from which the bow could be seen jutting out.

Despite their wretched condition, continues Starkie, these fiddles responded 'as if they possessed in the grain of their wood a particle of that magic which gave to the Cremonas their golden tone'. No matter how badly a gypsy might play, once he became excited by the audience to do his best, then he could make his instrument resound 'with a wild untutored music'. All that he did was the result of intuition and tradition; printed music was to him a marvel which he had never learnt to read.

Talking of Cremona, the violinist's Mecca, there are thousands of violins labelled with the name of 'Stradivari', 'Amati', 'Guarneri' or of some other gifted old maker who worked in that city, and the ignorant finding one fondly imagine they have within their grasp a potential fortune. But labels are cheap and are no evidence that an instrument is a genuine 'old master'. It may mean merely that a certain model shape has been followed.

In Scotland, a hundred years ago, there was a maker who acquired a facility in rattling up instruments out of poor wood, and with hardly any tools. The violins he produced, an attractive pale yellow in colour, were built to look like a heavy, deep Stradivarius, and were so labelled. He would pawn them and then get his wife to dispose of the ticket to some unwary player.

It took longer in England than elsewhere in Europe for violinists to be well regarded. Samuel Butler in *Hudibras*, his mock epic satirizing the Puritans, wrote about a man who became a professional fiddler:

> A squeaking engine he apply'd
> Unto his neck on north-east side ...
> His grisly beard was long and thick,
> With which he strung his fiddle-stick;

For he to horse tail scorned to owe,
For what on his own chin did grow.

Louis XIV had a celebrated band of violins led by Lully, and
Charles II, on returning to England from exile in France, followed
his example and started a similar one of twenty-four violins. The
status of violinists improved as a result, thus remedying the
injustice caused by an ordinance issued in Oliver Cromwell's time
declaring that anyone caught 'fiddling or making music in any inn,
alehouse, or tavern, or proffering themselves, or desiring, or
entreating any person or persons to hear them play shall be
adjudged rogues, vagabonds, and sturdy beggars'.

In the actual year of Charles II's restoration to the throne,
Anthony Wood of Oxford University wrote of chamber music
there:

The Gentlemen in private meeting which I frequented played three, four
and five parts with viols, a treble viol, tenor viol, counter-tenor and bass,
with an organ, virginal or harpsicon joined with them; and they esteemed a
violin to be an instrument only belonging to a common fiddler, and could
not endure that it should come among them for fear of making their
meetings to be vain and fidling.

Old prejudices take long to perish, and we find Jonathan Swift
mentioning how he hurried away when a certain man approached
him. 'He was a fiddler, and consequently a rogue,' explained the
Irish Dean. A modern writer with similar sentiments, Oliver
Herford, suggested that perhaps it was because Nero played the
fiddle that the people burned Rome. Incidentally, whatever it was
that Nero played it was not a violin, as they did not exist at that
time.

But even when violinists, thanks to continued royal patronage,
became regarded as respectable, there were still those who
objected to the sound itself. According to Alfred Bendiner in
Music In My Eyes, a man should not attend a violin concert
'unless he's lost his dog . . . or if there is any real reason to have a
good cry'.

The violinist practising at home provides free entertainment for
his neighbours who otherwise might have to pay to hear him
playing at concerts. In 1878, a 'silent violin' was invented by

Gebrüder Wolff of Kreuznach. Unlike the so-called dumb pianoforte, which has a keyboard but no sounding mechanism, it was not absolutely silent, but its volume of tone was so considerably reduced that, although perfectly audible to the performer, it did not penetrate the walls of his room.

The alternative to entertaining the neighbours is to play where they cannot hear. There have been students, of course, who, forbidden to practise in their bedsitters, have done so in the streets or underground, thus earning the money to pay their rents.

Fritz Kreisler wrote with great perception about the violin, stressing that it is the player who produces the tone, and defining a good instrument as one that puts the least impediment in the way of expression. But for all that, a violin was not simply wood and catgut.

It has moods, and must be wooed. It selects, gives itself to one and withholds itself from another. . . . Hardly a violin, even among the supreme specimens, does not have a weak strain somewhere, and the master's task is to hide that strain. . . There are fiddles that are beautiful physically, and that reach great heights on occasion, and yet are not dependable. They are outlaws, rogues that love you one moment and betray you the next with some wolf-tone. . . . Such a violin is like a horse that won't be ridden, or ridden only by certain masters and on certain days.

On another occasion, Kreisler pointed out that violins were as sensitive as humans; like them, they tire and need a rest now and then. He always gave his best ones a rest of at least six months.

Kreisler had many talents. One was for card tricks. After he had been entertaining the guests at a soirée in this way, one of them asked if he would be willing to perform in his home. 'All bookings are made through my agent,' Kreisler replied.

The guest took him literally, the night of the party arrived and Kreisler appeared with his Stradivarius. The host looked at it and exclaimed: 'Good heavens, so you can play the fiddle, too.'

On another occasion, a New York social climber was told by Kreisler that his fee for giving a violin recital in her house would be $1000. When agreeing to this, she stipulated that he must not mix with her friends. 'In that case,' he returned, 'I shall charge you only $500.'

Viola

Catherine Drinker Bowen in her book *Friends and Fiddlers* says that she never knew a viola player who was not modest, as well as being a good musician with a working knowledge of two or three instruments. Most of them were former fiddlers. 'I wasn't good enough on the violin,' a violist would tell one. 'I couldn't play those high notes up by the bridge.' Mrs Bowen thought that viola-playing eliminated the ego, 'even the virulent malignant male ego', and, as far as ensemble was concerned, it admitted no exhibitionism. A viola was more than a large violin. It had a different quality requiring a different technique from that of the violin which made it very difficult for violinists to master the instrument.

The viola is the backbone of string quartets, Mrs Bowen continues.

Your violist has, as a rule, neither melody nor bass; he can hear everything that goes on. When he has the melody, it is heavenly; one asks oneself in awe, 'Is the instrument itself responsible for such a tone, or is it the skilled *vibrato* of that left hand?' When the viola plays bass, the ensemble, lacking the cello's deep finality, has another quality, a strange, tremulous something that projects us, at once into an unknown place, into a fourth auditory dimension, a fascinating Erewhon full of half lights, half sounds; of breaths, as it were, half-drawn.

Mrs Bowen thought the viola, as the perfect instrument of ensemble, ideal for the married woman. It was the alto voice – 'its spirit that of sturdy, self-respecting subordination'. She had known three very satisfactory violists who were also extremely satisfactory as wives, and this was despite the fact that on the face of it the viola did not appear to be a woman's instrument, being large and bulky and requiring strong fingers to produce the right tone together with considerable muscular endurance to sustain it. In fact, one of the three wives in question, a powerful woman, confessed that her shoulder was lame for a week after she had played in an amateur string quartet. But that only made her more determined to master the instrument, which she did. Another of those wives also had trouble at the start, for, according to Mrs Bowen: 'She went, indeed, at the viola. She tore it to pieces; not before or since have I heard a viola emit such crucifying sounds. Mrs Van Bart suffered from these sounds as much as any of us, for she was truly musical, but she never apologized. She made faces, she drew on her breath through her teeth, but she never apologized.' Mr Van Bart, a professional musician, who conducted the quartet in his country house, would patiently tell his spouse to play the notes evenly, not to hurry, and 'not to be gasping for breath like a hookèd trout'. It sounds like the sort of playing Sir Thomas Beecham had in mind when he remarked: 'If you had heard the violas when I was young, you'd take a bismuth tablet.'

Others have expressed similar sentiments to those of Catherine Drinker Bowen. 'The viola,' wrote Albert Cavignac, 'is a philosopher, sad, helpful, always ready to come to the aid of others, but reluctant to call attention to himself.' Harry Ellis Dickson, after 30 years with the Boston Symphony Orchestra, considered that violists were the least troublesome of players. 'They don't even resent being looked upon by their violin colleagues as broken-down fiddlers. There was a time when the viola section of an orchestra was made up of the oldest men and any player under sixty would be looked upon with great sympathy.'

Dickson relates how, at a concert conducted by Koussevitzsky at the Sanders Theatre of Cambridge, USA, the bow of one of the viola players, Lehner, flew out of his hand during a brisk *tremolo* passage into the lap of a lady in the first row. Fortunately for him, Koussevitzky did not notice this and Lehner, managing to keep calm, went on miming his *tremolo* as if he still held a bow. A few bars later, when the conductor turned to another section of the orchestra, the woman quickly handed it back to the much relieved violist.

In common with other musicians immersed in their art, some viola players have not the time to spare to learn much about what goes on in the world beyond their sphere of interest. Frank Sinatra, having attended a concert given by the Boston Symphony Orchestra, went to visit a player friend afterwards. As the two men were leaving, they encountered Jean Le Franc, the principal violist. 'Do you know Frank Sinatra?' asked the latter's companion.

'Of course I know the Franck Sonata,' returned Le Franc. 'But who is this?'

Nowadays viola players receive the recognition they deserve. As Bernard Shore, himself a brilliant violist, has written in *The Orchestra Speaks*:

For generations the first violins have been the spoilt darlings of the orchestra, and the cellos, though less spoilt, have usually had plenty of 'fat', but the violas and the second violins of the early days of Haydn and Mozart, to say nothing of Bach and Handel, might have been members of the Plumbers' and Stonemasons' Guilds, and musicians only in their spare time, so seldom were they trusted out of shallow water.

This was still true even in 1869, when Wagner wrote:

The viola is commonly (with rare exceptions) played by infirm violinists, or by decrepit players of wind instruments who happen to have been acquainted with a string instrument once upon a time; at best a competent viola player occupies the first desk, so that he may play the occasional solo for that instrument; but I have seen even this function performed by the leader of the first violins.

Cello

'The cello is like a beautiful woman,' Pablo Casals has said, 'who has not grown older but younger with time, more slender, more supple, more graceful.'

Cellists, like conductors, have been called prima donnas. Harry Ellis Dickson in *Gentlemen More Dolce Please*, his delightfully 'Irreverent Memories of Thirty Years in the Boston Symphony Orchestra', said in his comparison of cellists and divas that the former were super-sensitive, conceited, quarrelsome, and that if one discovered two who spoke to each other, things were going quite well.

An English musician, Thomas Russell, in his *Philharmonic: A Future for the Symphony Orchestra*, had somewhat similar views. Cellists were 'incorrigible individualists, each considering himself a soloist, and perhaps quite rightly. The singing, sentimental quality of the instrument has its counterpart in a rather romantic view of life. An untidy cellist is an exception, and their smart clothes, a certain loquacity, and good looks, often endear them to the fair sex.'

Bernard Shore, in *The Orchestra Speaks*, claimed that, in his experience, the cello department, though irresponsible, provided 'more humour and cheerful spirits than all the other members of the family put together'. He believed that a cellist must have a sense of humour, 'seeing that he has to spend most of his waking hours leaning over a long box'.

Catherine Drinker Bowen, the American author of *Friends and Fiddlers,* shared Bernard Shore's view of a cellist needing to have a sense of humour and being inevitably good-natured. Otherwise, he would not have contracted for a lifetime of walking along crowded streets and travelling by public transport 'in company with that elephantine bundle'. Mrs Bowen, herself a violinist, says admiringly: 'Watch a cellist tuck his instrument under his arm on a snowy night, hear him declare cheerily that he doesn't need a lift.' She thought that 'as queer as a cellist' was no idle simile. In her experience, cellists as a class were almost impossible to crush and she wondered whether this might be due to their 'essential unassailable guilelessness'. Good cellists were 'as scarce as charity'.

Cellists who swayed as they played did not annoy Mrs Bowen, but she was well aware that they drove other listeners to fury. Excessive swaying in any fiddle was distracting and made one suspect 'pose, ultra-temperament'. She herself had been brought up in the old school which placed a china plate under the right foot of every aspiring fiddler so the victim could not sway 'but must needs remain perched horribly upon an exhausted left leg'. A friend of hers once attended a concert in Paris where the cellist rocked in his chair like a lightship. Wider and wider grew the diameter of his sweep until a voice from the balcony called mildly, without rancour: '*Mais repose-toi, mon enfant! Repose-toi, pour l'amour de Dieu!*'

According to Harry Ellis Dickson, cellists hated bass players and when Sergei Koussevitzky became conductor of the Boston Philharmonic, knowing that he had been a bass virtuoso, the cellists regarded him with disdain. Soon after his arrival, the basses invited him to play for them, which, with some reluctance, he did. Afterwards, a cellist told his wife: 'It was astounding! I never heard such bass playing. I closed my eyes and said to myself: "That is not a bass – it sounds like a lousy cello!"'

Shore, too, talks of conflict between bass players and cellists. The relationship was good-humoured, with each affecting slight contempt of the other. He gives an example of the sort of verbal exchanges that might occur, with the basses saying: 'You cellos think that because a passage is easy for your rotten instrument, it is the same for us. We want a lot of bow for that.' To which, the cellists would retort: 'All right, do it your own way, if you must play on a thing that no dog would like to use.'

That great cellist Paul Tortellier, interviewed by John Duarte in *Records and Recording* for June, 1977, mentioned some of the difficulties faced by cellists. The gut strings of their instruments being bigger than those of the violin, they were more difficult to get into resonance, into motion. It was possible for them to whistle – 'if you miss the note, it will sound two octaves higher'. It was more difficult to play the cello where there was humidity, for the hair on the bow would bite the string less. Bernard Shaw once described a bad cellist as sounding like 'a bee buzzing in a stone jug'.

Gerald Moore, the pianist, speaking from personal observation, concluded that to acquire a big tone became a fetish with some cellists and 'often like singers forcing their voices they gain it only at the expense of quality'. He also claimed that the deeper-voiced cello can easily be outweighed by the pianoforte. The celebrated cellist Piatigorsky once complained about this. After recording a sonata with Schnabel at the piano, and then listening to the result, he said: 'The only way to record with Schnabel is to put the cello up against the microphone and record the piano from Paris.'

However, Schnabel was not pleased either. His comment, after listening independently, was 'Of course, with His Master's Voice it seems to be a tradition that the piano should never be heard.'

'Walter, is there someone else?'

Double-bass

In the early eighteenth century, Benedetto Marcello wrote in jest that the double-bass player should play sitting down and wearing gloves, need not tune the lowest string of his instrument, should apply rosin to the upper half of the bow only, and could safely put away his instrument and go home when the third act of an opera is half over. That advice would certainly not be relevant to modern players, for as Bernard Shore with his long experience has written: 'The basses are the most spectacular in their preparation, and almost blatant in spit and polish and the general grooming of their charges.' But even up to the middle of last century double-bass-playing was generally not of a high standard. Berlioz has recorded that for some time it was usual when performing the passage for cellos and basses in the *Scherzo* of Beethoven's Fifth Symphony to omit the latter at the Paris Conservatoire concerts, leaving the former to play on their own.

In 1844 a festival was held at the Industrial Exhibition in Paris and Berlioz mustered a monster orchestra containing thirty-six basses. He wrote of their performance at a rehearsal: 'When we came to the *Scherzo*, it was like the grunting of about fifty ferocious pigs. Such was the incoherence and want of precision.'

One of the greatest of double-bass virtuosi was Giovanni Bottesini, whose heyday was in the middle of the last century when he played with the Royal Philharmonic at the Hanover Square Rooms. The Rev. Hugh Haweis has left these vivid impressions of him:

A tall, sallow-looking creature with a black moustache and straight hair, with long bony fingers, yet withal a comely hand. . . . How he bewildered

us by playing all sorts of melodies in flute-like harmonies, as though he
had a hundred nightingales caged in his double-bass! Where he got his
harmonic sequences from; how he hit the exact place with his long,
sensitive, ivory-looking fingers; how he swarmed up and down the finger-
board, holding it round the neck at times with the grip of a giant, then, after
eliciting a grumble of musical thunder, darting up to the top and down
again, with an expression on his face that never seemed to alter, and his
face always calmly and rather grimly surveying the audience; how his bow
moved with the rapidity of lightning, and his fingers seemed like Miss
Kilmansegg's leg to be a judicious compound of clockwork and steam; all
this, and more, is now a matter of musical history.

Thomas Russell in *Philharmonic* suggested that the ideal
double-bass player should be tall, broad and muscular, and a
match for the massive wooden structure of which he is master. As
a race, he had found them having more respect for their
instruments than any other string players. Perhaps it was because
they had frequently to be craftsmen, busily applying their skill
when their unwieldy instruments met with accidents in transit.

Toscanini once reprimanded a bass soloist at his entry in
Beethoven's Ninth for singing his note values too precisely. 'Why
do you sing so correct? It must be *rubato, rubato, rubato!* Sing it
freely! Who told you to sing it so correct?'

'Well, maestro, as a matter of fact it was Koussevitzky.'

'Bah! That double-bass player!' exclaimed Toscanini contemptuously. His instrument, of course, was the cello.

'One only, mate!'

Flute

'Flute, *n*. A variously perforated hollow stick intended for the punishment of sin,' is how Ambrose Bierce begins his disapproving definition. Centuries earlier, Theophrastus wrote: 'The sound of the flute will cure epilepsy and sciatic gout.'

Harry Ellis Dickson is much kinder. According to him, the dandies of any orchestra are the flute players, being the best-dressed, the quietest, the most gentlemanly and the easiest to get along with. Not only that, playing the least troublesome of all instruments and having no reed, mouthpiece or string problems, they are normally the best adjusted members of a symphony orchestra and the most affluent on account of the constant demand for flute lessons.

There were, however, certain professional hazards in the past. New York's old Metropolitan became increasingly dilapidated, with its electric wiring frayed and exposed. During a performance, Frederick Wilkins, a flautist in the orchestra, had a long rest in his part, so he placed his silver flute on the side of the stage nearest to him. Suddenly, there was a blinding flash and the instrument rapidly melted before he realized what had happened.

Conductors often behave as though they are conversant with every instrument in the orchestra. James Galway relates in his memoirs how Sir Malcolm Sargent once tried, using his baton, to demonstrate how he wished him to play a certain passage. Galway wished he could have photographed the great man who played his 'flute' with all the keys on the wrong side.

This virtuoso flautist adds that Sargent once told him about a man he came across in a Cairo street playing just three notes on the flute. When the conductor returned six months later, the fellow

90

was still playing the same three notes, so Sir Malcolm asked him why.

'Because everybody is busy looking for these notes,' was the reply, 'and I'm the only one who has found them.'

'I gather that you play the piccolo, Mr. Mountebank.'

Oboe

According to Harry Ellis Dickson's amusingly irreverent comments on his fellow musicians, oboists were the unhappiest of players, continually regretting their lot in being saddled with such a fickle, perfidious instrument. Most of their time was spent shaving their double-reeds. Now and then an oboist would attach the reed to his pursed lips and blow, only with inevitable dissatisfaction to start shaving it again. 'On the stage the oboist is the most detached member of the orchestra and the most fidgety.'

If the oboe section were closely watched at a concert, Dickson claimed, one would notice 'constant activity completely unrelated to the music'. Whenever there was more than a bar's rest, the reed would be removed, inspected, cursed, then put back just in time for the next entrance.

Between movements the reed is shaved with the trusty knife that lies next to every oboe player. While the music is going on, the oboists confer with one another, thump their instruments, blow through the keys with a hissing sound to remove the water, and generally behave as though there is no concert. . . . To the first-class oboist the over-all continuity of a composition means nothing. His world consists of turning out musical phrases in tune, in rhythm, and with good sound. The rest is not his concern.

As for the first oboist, Dickson continues, he and the conductor did not usually speak to each other, and he detested most of all string players. 'He gives his "A" to the orchestra a quarter tone flat, convinced that in a short time they will sabotage him by playing sharp anyway. For some reason, all first oboists are gangsters. They are tough, irascible, double-reed roosters, feared by colleagues and conductors.'

Grattan Cooke, leading oboist with the Philharmonic in the second quarter of the last century, once arrived in the concert room with a long ladder. According to Sterndale-Bennett, 'He had resented the introduction of a very high note for his oboe in a new composition, and had gone for assistance to enable him to reach it.'

Artur Nikisch, writing as an experienced conductor, pointed out that oboists (and bassoonists) had to blow into a narrow reed in such a way that a large amount of air stayed stored in the chest to be released carefully and slowly. This, he said, made the blood rise to the brain, rendering them so nervous that conductors ought to be extremely tactful when speaking to them.

Sir Thomas Beecham in *A Mingled Chime* described the bass oboe as an instrument for which there are few to praise and very few to love. Delius had included an important solo part for one in the score of his *Dance Rhapsody*, first performed at a Three Choirs Festival concert in Gloucester Cathedral. Beecham thought it extraordinary how such a piece had come to be chosen for performance in a cathedral – 'nothing except possibly the anarchic operations of a swing band would have been less appropriate'. The organizers had blundered further in persuading the composer to allow the solo to be played by a young lady oboist of semi-amateur status who had volunteered at short notice to see what she could do with it.

Beecham comments:

Now the bass oboe, like certain other members of the single- and double-reed families, is to be endured only if manipulated with supreme cunning and control; otherwise its presence in the orchestra is a strain upon the nervous system of conductor and players alike, a danger to the seemly rendering of the piece in hand and a cause of astonishment and risibility in the audience. A perfect breath control is the essential requisite for keeping it well in order and this alone can obviate the eruption of sounds that would arouse attention even in a circus. As none of these safety-first precautions had been taken, the public, which had assembled in the sombre interior of an eleventh-century basilica in anticipation of some pensive and poetical effect from the most discussed musician of the day, was confounded by the frequent audition of noises that resembled nothing so much as the painful endeavour of an anguished mother-duck to effect the speedy evacuation of an abnormally large-sized egg.

If Delius, who also conducted, had not been so celebrated and so respectable in appearance, continues Sir Thomas, he had often shuddered to think what might have happened. 'As it was, so successful proved the enterprise of the ministers of Momus that the wife of one of the leading ecclesiastical dignitaries precipitately fleeing the church decided it was better to absent herself from any of the subsequent performances rather than run the risk of losing a hardly won reputation for dignity and decorum.'

Clarinet

Possibly the worst disaster than can befall a clarinettist is for water to get into the instrument. James Galway, the flautist, tells in his reminiscences how during a concert given by the London Philharmonic at Red Rocks, Colorado, Roy Jarrett somehow managed to do this: when he blew his instrument the result was so funny that the entire orchestra, together with the huge audience, laughed uproariously and the second clarinettist was unable to take over.

Isaac Goldberg in *Tin Pan Alley* describes the clarinet's sound as being a 'leering cacherination', while Ambrose Bierce must have been scared by a clarinet when a baby or have lost a sweetheart to a charmer playing one, for he denounces the instrument as one 'of torture operated by a person with cotton in his ear' and adds: 'There are two instruments worse than a clarinet – two clarinets!'

Harry Ellis Dickson is not too complimentary about clarinet players; he describes them as 'the classic cry-babies of any orchestra' who 'look down their noses at any kind of vibrato, making it very difficult for them to play in tune (which they don't).' Always hunting in vain for a good reed, they imagined the conductor was constantly persecuting them.

Of all conductors, Arthur Nikisch was probably the most sympathetic towards clarinettists, for he maintained that they were inclined to be sentimental and must be addressed with 'infinite gentleness'.

Brass

Mozart as a child fainted, it is said, under the intolerable blare of the trumpet. Perhaps the man who caused this had taken in sport the advice of the Venetian satirist Benedetto Marcello to play out of tune and produce a perpetual *crescendo*. Harry Ellis Dickson tells us that the majority of trumpeters he knew were 'handsome, debonair and dashing' – and bachelors ('or should be') – whilst horn players were rebels, always agitating for more pay and less work, 'able to convince conductors that their lips could stand so much (or so little playing), and most symphony orchestras have double platoons'.

Rossini's operatic innovations in his *Otello* appealed to the public but upset the old school of musicians. Sigismondi of the Naples Conservatore was appalled when he examined the score. 'Rossini is mad!' he cried. 'The greatest of our composers have always been content with two horns. Five! They are enough to blow us to perdition!'

Donizetti, Sigismondi's pupil, relates how he was looking through the music of *Semiramide* in the library of Naples when the maestro came in and, peering over his shoulder, enquired: 'Who has composed this?'

'Rossini,' Donizetti replied.

Sigismondi read: 'Trumpets 1 2 3.' Aghast, he pressed his hands against his ears and groaned: 'One hundred and twenty-three trumpets – whatever next!' In spite of this, Rossini carried on writing parts for three trumpets.

'The timbre of the trombone is in its nature majestic and imposing,' approved Albert Lavignac. 'It is sufficiently powerful to dominate an orchestra and produces an impression of superhuman

96

power. . . . It can become terrible or mournful and full of dismay; or it may have the serenity of the organ. It is a superb instrument of lofty dramatic power, which should be reserved for great occasions.'

Sir Thomas Beecham was less complimentary about the instrument. He once asked a trombonist: 'Are you producing as much sound as possible from that quaint and antique drainage system which you are applying to your face?'

Tuba players were regarded by Dickson as the loneliest of instrumentalists, morose and silent except when they sang to themselves, whilst Peter de Vries in *The Glory of the Hummingbird* described the tuba as 'certainly the most intestinal of instruments, the very lower bowel of music'. Bernard Shore quotes a player who complained: 'I should like a pound for every quart of air I've pumped into this radiator just warming it up. I'm exhausted before the concert.'

Such an attitude deserves sympathy when one considers the tuba's length – that built for John Philip Sousa's band measured 39 feet from oomp to pah. In Sydney as a guest conductor, Malcolm Sargent was horrified when he noticed that a player had sprayed his tuba with 'silver frost' to avoid having to polish so much tubing. 'Heavens!' Sargent exclaimed. 'What's that made of? Cardboard?'

'This weather, I daren't leave it off.'

A Lift for the Horn

In 1974 when the London Symphony Orchestra was rehearsing Benjamin Britten's *Serenade* in Bonn with André Previn as conductor the players had trouble in attaining the right effect at the end, when the French horn is meant to leave the stage for an unaccompanied moment during which the sound becomes increasingly faint. Then Barry Tuckwell, the horn virtuoso, tried standing in a goods lift and playing from there. Previn was delighted with the result and it was arranged that Tuckwell should take up the same position for the actual performance that evening, when the *diminuendo* proved even more impressive than at the rehearsal.

The audience's ovation could not have been more appreciative. Delighted, Previn signalled for Tuckwell to appear, but he could not be found. Whilst they waited, conductor, tenor, entire orchestra took bows in turn, then suddenly the panting virtuoso ran on to the stage and acknowledged the applause.

In the wings later, Tuckwell explained what had happened. 'I've been trying to find my way up from the basement. Somebody rang for the bloody lift just as I started the *diminuendo*. I hope you could hear it.' And, of course, Previn was able to tell him that in fact the mishap was the best thing that could have happened.

Bass Drum

'What have Rossini and Napoleon in common?' jested those who disliked the composer's music. To this, the answer was: 'Nothing – except in the noise which they made in Europe. They were both fond of employing the drum.'

A man once called on the composer asking for his help in obtaining a post in an orchestra. He said he played the drum. Hoping to get rid of the unwelcome visitor, Rossini replied that he could not possibly hear and judge him, not having that instrument in his house.

'Oh, I brought one with me. It's in the hall. May I fetch it?' persisted the visitor.

Rossini reluctantly agreed and, settling himself in an armchair, asked what the other was going to play.

'Your own overture to *Semiramide.*'

The very first bar of this contains a *tremolo* for the drum. Once he had performed this, the musician said: 'Now I have a rest of 78 bars, which, of course, I will skip.'

'Oh, no,' Rossini hurriedly objected, 'by all means count the 78 bars – I particularly want to hear those.'

In Rossini's time, the size of drums was limited by the dimensions of skins available in one piece to stretch across the heads. When in 1939 Verdi's *Macbeth* was staged at Glyndebourne, it was announced that the biggest bass drum in the world, six feet in diameter, had been specially built so that the thunder would have a more musical sound. This had taken a year to make, the firm of Henry Potter and Co. having had difficulty in finding two cow-hides large enough (a problem which no longer exists now that materials such as sheet plastic are obtainable). The enormous bass drum in Disneyland has its heads covered with this and its diameter is ten-and-a-half feet. The risk with huge drums is that they could explode through internal resonances being caused by the beating.

Orchestras are rather like congregations, and the conductor is like the parson who usually has the last word. A drummer in his fifties from the North of England was criticized by Otto Klemperer for getting into a rhythmic cul-de-sac at a rehearsal. 'Look 'ere, Dr Klemperer,' he protested, 'I've been counting my bars for 30 years.'

'And how many have you counted so far?' scowled the conductor.

On the other hand, the young drummer attending his first rehearsal with Sir Thomas Beecham might in view of his inexperience have been expected to blunder. He was all keyed up, knowing he had one of the percussion player's scarce solos to attempt.

'How does Sir Thomas like it?' he enquired nervously.

'Hot and strong,' asserted the bassoon. 'You can't give him too much. And remember, he's an old man now – getting a bit deaf.'

Beecham bustled in and the rehearsal commenced. He at once focussed his attention on the new recruit, whom he had never previously met. 'Let us start with the drum solo,' he decided.

The youth, eager to impress, attacked his drums with frenzied ferocity whilst Sir Thomas watched with assumed astonishment. 'Young man,' he commented as the shattering racket ended, 'you're not a drummer – you're an anarchist.'

Identifying a Musician

Apart from his amusing comments on the idiosyncrasies of instrumentalists, Harry Ellis Dickson provided in his book *Gentlemen, More Dolce Please* some useful tips for sleuths examining a body suspected to be that of a musician. If it should have calluses on the fingers of the left hand then it must be that of a string player. A violinist would also have a mark under his left chin; a viola player would have a somewhat larger one. A corpse with a callus on the left thumb in addition to those on the fingers must be that of a cellist, a deduction that would be confirmed if the deceased bore a red mark on his chest caused by pressing the cello towards him. A double-bass player would have outsize hands, with bigger calluses on the right one, due to slapping the strings.

All clarinettists bore on the inside of their left thumbs their own type of callus through bearing instruments upon it. A harpist could be easily identified by the calluses on all fingers except the little ones, which were never employed. As for double-reed players such as oboists and bassoonists, Dickson pointed out that their occupational hallmark was a raw irritation on the inside of their lips, brought about through rubbing against the teeth; and lastly, brass players could be spotted by their elongated upper lips.

'Show' Pianists

There is an Italian proverb that he who plays the piano keeps sane, while Bernard Shaw wrote in the *Fortnightly Review* for February, 1894: 'The pianoforte is the most important of all musical instruments: its invention was to music what the invention of printing was to poetry.' Yet until the early nineteenth century a piano was, as Leigh Hunt put it, little more than 'a harp in a box'.

Jan Ládislav Dussek (1760–1812) was responsible for staging spectacular piano-playing to the best advantage. Having a perfect profile, and being rather vain, he decided to sit exhibiting his right side to his admirers. This had the additional merits of exposing to view the bow of the piano, whilst its raised lid served to direct the sound straight into the auditorium. He also had the bright idea of rubbing his hands whenever necessary in the bran which he kept hidden in his coat pockets.

'*Le beau Dussek*', as he was called, was also the first to make the use of the pedal an art, and to play a six-octave piano, a Broadwood, in public. His fellow countryman, the pianist Tomaschek, describes a concert given at Prague in 1804 by the maestro from Bohemia as follows:

After the few opening bars of his first solo, the audience uttered one general "Oh!" There was in fact something magical about the way in which Dussek with all his charming grace of manner, through his wonderful touch, extracted from the instrument delicious and at the same time emphatic tones. His fingers were like a company of ten singers endowed with equal executive power and able to produce with the utmost perfection whatever their director would require.

Dussek's main rival was J.B. Cramer, whom Beethoven praised as 'the only pianist of his time, all the rest count for nothing'. He was an inveterate snuff-taker. Ignaz Moscheles wrote of him:

My good housekeeper maintains that after every visit of the great master, the floor must be cleaned of the snuff he has spilt; while I, as a piano player, cannot forgive him for disfiguring his aristocratic, long, thin fingers, with their beautifully shaped nails, by the use of it and often clogging the action of the keys.

Piano-playing was never quite the same again after Beethoven. Compared with his playing, that of his predecessors must have sounded, as Harold Schonberg has put it, like 'the trickle of a rivulet' against 'the surge of the ocean'. The pianos of his day had not been built to withstand such execution, and as a result he ruined more than any other player of his day. Anton Reicha, who turned pages for the composer when he was playing a Mozart concerto at court, related: 'But I was mostly occupied in wrenching the strings . . . which snapped, while the hammers stuck among the broken strings. Beethoven insisted on finishing the concerto, and so back and forth I leaped, jerking out a string, disentangling a hammer, turning a page, and I worked harder than him.'

This probably occurred in 1796, when Beethoven was using a Streicher piano. That same year he wrote to the piano manufacturer complaining: 'There is no doubt that as far as the manner of playing it is concerned, the pianoforte is still the least studied and least developed of all instruments: often one thinks that one is merely listening to a harp . . . I hope that the time will come when the harp and the pianoforte will be treated as entirely different instruments.'

Some 22 years later, Beethoven's dream was fulfilled when John Broadwood sent him a superb grand piano with a range of over six octaves. The composer was enraptured and used it for the rest of his life. Unfortunately, he was becoming increasingly deaf. He had always been heavy-handed, responsible for breakage after breakage, and often clumsily knocking the contents of his inkwell into the piano. Owing to his loss of hearing, he banged out more and more wrong notes.

Ludwig Spohr records that he only once heard Beethoven play the piano. This was quite accidentally during a rehearsal of a new Trio in D major in his apartment. It was no pleasure because the piano was out of tune, which did not worry the maestro at all since he could not hear it. Moreover little was left of his once celebrated virtuosity. In *forte* passages he hit the keys so hard that the strings rattled, and in *piano* passages played so softly that whole groups of notes never sounded at all, with the result that it was impossible to follow even with the piano score as a guide.

Anton Felix Schindler, Beethoven's private secretary, has written that the composer was especially fond of sitting at his piano in the twilight and improvising. Sometimes he would play the violin or viola that he always kept on it.

For the other people in the house his playing especially of the string instruments which he was unable to tune, was agony to the ears. His extemporizing on the piano was seldom intelligible, for it was usually extremely agitated. Generally the lack of clarity was caused by the left hand being spread wide and laid upon the keyboard so heavily that the noise would drown the much softer playing of the right hand.

Schindler revealed that in Beethoven's last years the piano manufacturer Conrad Graf made him a sounding-board which when placed on the piano was intended to conduct the sound of the notes to his ears more effectively. The device worked well for single notes, but 'full chords completely overwhelmed the maestro's ear, since the air waves, confined within a very limited space must have had a deafening effect'.

Johann Andreas Stumpff, an instrument-maker, called on Beethoven near the end of his life and examined the Broadwood. 'Quite a sight confronted me,' he wrote. 'The upper registers were mute, and the broken strings in a tangle, like a thorn bush whipped by a storm.'

Sir John Russell, who also visited Beethoven, painted a vivid word picture of his becoming completely unconscious that there was anything else in existence once he sat down at the piano. 'The muscles of his face swell and its veins stand out; the wild eye rolls doubly wild, the mouth quivers; and Beethoven looks like a wizard overpowered by the demons he has called up. . . . When playing softly, he does not bring out a single note. He hears it himself in his mind's ear. . . . The instrument is actually as dumb as the musician is deaf.'

Schindler, who served as amanuensis and factotum as well as secretary, throws amusing light on another side of his maestro's character, stating that washing and bathing were among the most pressing necessities of his life.

In this respect he was indeed an Oriental: to his way of thinking Mohammed did not exaggerate a whit in the number of ablutions he prescribed. If he did not dress to go out in the morning working hours, he would stand in great *déshabillé* at his wash basin and pour large pitchers of water over his hands, bellowing up and down the scale or sometimes humming loudly to himself. Then he would stride around his room with rolling or staring eyes, jot something down, then resume his pouring of water and loud singing. There were moments of deep meditation, to which no one could have objected but for two unfortunate consequences. First of all, the servants would often burst out laughing. This made the master angry and he would sometimes assault them in language that made him cut an even more ridiculous figure.

Or, secondly, he would come into conflict with the landlord, for all too often so much water was spilled that it went right through the floor. This was one of the main reasons for Beethoven's unpopularity as a tenant. The floor of his living-room would have had to be covered with asphalt to prevent all that water from seeping through. And the master was totally unaware of the excess of inspiration under his feet!

It may surprise some to learn that Beethoven, according to Schindler, loved buffoonery and practical joking. He relates how the wife of a pianist longed to have a lock from the composer's crown, so for a prank he sent her some hairs from the beard of a goat, actually not too different from his own coarse grey hair. The admirer boasted about this far and wide, but eventually the truth came out and her husband, very much aggrieved, wrote to the great man accusing him of having insulted the lady. Beethoven, feeling rather guilty, atoned by sacrificing a large piece of his hair and sending it to her with a note begging forgiveness.

Piano-playing became the rage of Europe with the rise to fame of the incomparable Liszt. The king of the Romantics, he would throw his hands up into the air from the keyboard, twist and turn and leap and lunge. His was bravura playing that no one else could surpass. Apart from Beethoven, he was the first to break away from the old technique of keeping one's hands as near to the keys as possible and the first to 'orchestrate' on the piano.

Women flung their jewellery at him, and instead of his kissing their hands, they kissed his finger-tips. They clawed at each other fighting to acquire as souvenirs broken strings and hammers from the pianos he wrecked or to steal one of the green doe-skin gloves he peeled from his shapely white hands and tossed with deliberate carelessness on the floor before commencing to play. One admirer cut out a piece of material covering the very spot on a couch where he had sat; another retrieved the dregs of his tea and poured them into a vial to keep as a sacred relic. Two Hungarian countesses tore each other's elegant toilettes to rags battling for his snuff-box, whilst a mature matron salvaged the stub of cigar he had been smoking and kept it in her bosom for life. 'I saw ladies eyeing him as though they would like to eat the last shred of his Abbé's robe,' said the composer Grieg, after a visit to Weimar.

The poet Heine, who witnessed some of these odd scenes, recorded how he asked a physician specializing in women's complaints why Liszt had such an effect on them. This expert thought such hysteria due to 'magnetism, galvanism and electricity' and 'contagion in a sultry hall filled with innumerable wax lights and hundreds of perfumed and perspiring people'. Heine goes on to say that the medical man spoke, too, of 'histrionic epilepsy, of the phenomenon of tickling, of musical cantharides, and other unmentionable matters'.

Until Liszt's time, musicians had been treated by royalty and the upper classes as very much their inferiors. Liszt behaved as though he was far superior to them. When King Frederick Wilhelm IV of Prussia presented him with diamonds, he contemptuously flung them into the wings. In Paris, disapproving of King Louis Philippe, he refused to play before him, while in Russia, when giving a recital before the Russian Court, he was annoyed to hear Czar Nicholas I talking loudly to his entourage. Liszt therefore ceased playing and sat with bowed head as if awaiting a command. At last, the Czar deigned to ask why the pianist had done this, and Liszt answered: 'Music herself should be silent when Nicholas speaks.'

Whilst a great deal of the Liszt furore was spontaneous, some was stage-managed. Heine, Liszt's contemporary, throws interesting light on the source of some of the floral tributes. He relates that the celebrated tenor Rubini undertook a tour with Liszt, sharing expenses and profits. The pianist went everywhere with his business manager and publicist Signor Bellini, who at the end of the tour prepared the accounts and handed a copy to Rubini. On examining this, the latter was staggered to find that among the joint expenses were listed quite large amounts for 'laurel wreaths', 'bouquets', 'laudatory poems', and 'miscellaneous ovation items'.

The naïve tenor had imagined that all these tokens of public favour had been gifts from genuine fans of his. Incensed, he refused to pay for the bouquets, which had largely consisted of costly camellias – Liszt's favourite flowers.

In 1835, a sensation was caused when Liszt fainted while giving a recital in Paris. This led to Oscar Commettant writing a satirical sketch, which aroused much amusement:

A certain great pianist, who is as clever a manager as he is an admirable performer, pays women at a rate of 25 francs per concert to pretend to faint away with pleasure in the middle of a fantasia taken at such a pace that it would have been humanly impossible to finish it. The pianist leaps from his instrument and rushes to the assistance of the poor fainting lady, while everybody in the room believed that, but for that accident, the prodigious pianist would have accomplished the miracle of all time at the keyboard.

It happened one night that a woman paid to faint forgot her cue and fell fast asleep. The pianist was playing Weber's *Concertstück*, and, relying on his accomplice to interrupt the piece's finale, he was attacking it in his usual break-neck manner. What could he do faced with such a crisis? Stumble and trip like a tenth-rate pianist, or pretend to be suddenly afflicted with loss of memory? No, he simply acted the part which the lady ought to have performed and fainted away himself.

People crowded around the pianist . . . They carried him into the green-room. The men applauded, the women wailed, and the lady who ought to have fainted woke up at last and promptly fainted, distressed at having failed to pretend to faint.

It is only natural of course, that artists as successful as Liszt should be denigrated by the envious, but there can be little doubt that, apart from being a consummate showman, he was the greatest pianist of all time. As Sir Charles Hallé has said: 'Anton Rubinstein spoke the truth when he said that in comparison with Liszt all other pianists are children.'

Alexander Dreyschock (1818–69) was Liszt's contemporary and in some ways a superior technician. By practising sixteen hours a day with his left hand on its own, he succeeded in playing octaves as smoothly and as swiftly as single-note passages. When J.B. Cramer heard him, he exclaimed in amazed admiration: 'The man has no left hand – they are both right hands.'

After attending Dreyschock's début in Paris, Heine wrote to a friend:

He makes a hell of a racket. One does not seem to hear one pianist but three score of them. Since on the evening of his concert, the wind was blowing south by west, perhaps you heard the tremendous sounds in Augsburg? At such a distance their effect must be agreeable. Here, however, in this Department of the Seine, one may easily burst an ear-drum when the piano-pounder thumps away. Go hang yourself, Franz Liszt! You are but an ordinary god in comparison with this god of thunder.

When Dreyschock first played before the Emperor of Austria, he started to perspire because the room was over-heated and all the windows were shut. Franz Josef I listened very attentively whilst eyeing him closely. On ending his performance, Dreyschock rose. Although he longed to take out his handkerchief and dab his face, he thought it best to wait till later for the Emperor was approaching. 'My dear Dreyschock,' he began, 'I have heard Moscheles play.' The pianist bowed. 'I have heard Thalberg.' Dreyschock bowed lower. 'I have heard Liszt.' The hero of left-hand octaves bowed very low indeed. 'I have heard all the great players.' The Emperor gave a smile. 'But I never, never saw anybody perspire as you do.' Years later, Benno Moiseiwitch often wore a blouse of black silk when playing to conceal the fact that he, too, perspired excessively.

The exploits of Liszt and the other pianists of the Romantic school created an insatiable appetite among the young to emulate them, and Heinrich Heine deplored the effects of the vogue in March, 1843, writing in his *Lutetia*:

For its sins, the ruling bourgeoisie must not only endure old classic tragedies and trilogies that are not classical, but . . . an even more horrible artistic treat, namely that pianoforte that one now can never anywhere escape, that one hears sounding in every house, in every company, day and night. Yes, pianoforte is the name of that instrument of torture . . . If only the innocent did not have to suffer as well! . . . (Oh, my wall neighbours, young English ladies, are at this moment playing a brilliant morçeau for two left hands.) Those shrill tinkle-tones without natural resonance, those heartless whirrings, that arch prosaic, rumbling and hacking, that forte-piano is killing all our thinking and feeling; we become stupid, dulled-off, imbecile. This predominance of piano playing, not to speak of the triumphal processions of the piano virtuosi, are characteristic of our time and bear witness to the victory of mechanism upon spirit. Technical proficiency, the precision of an automaton, self-identification with wired wood, the resounding instrumentalization of the human being, all this is now praised and celebrated as the highest of things . . .

Fashions, however, change. Towards the end of 1847, Liszt retired as a piano virtuoso. Public infatuation had reached its peak. It had been at its strongest with the bourgeoisie, but the revolutions that erupted throughout Europe in 1848 had by now exerted a far-reaching effect on their tastes. As Arthur Loesser has written: 'The virtuoso acrobat, pure and simple, was gradually being replaced by a performer who considered himself an interpreter.' Eleven years later, that astute Austrian critic Eduard Hanslick wrote in the *Wiener Presse* that quite a while had elapsed since the time when an accomplished pianist could show himself off 'like a rare bird', but though the demand for virtuosi had dropped, the number of young people trained to play the piano and seeking employment had never been higher. He asked:

What are they driving at, these many pianizing youths and maidens, that makes them concentrate such heavy advertising fire from the street corners upon the unwary passer-by? A gentle anxiety comes over me at the sight of all these names on white cards . . . Do they really hope to lure paying mortals hither, and by playing the piano to inspire a public that itself consists of nothing but piano players? . . .

In bitter seriousness: the sight of so many virtuoso announcements makes me sad . . . They are addressing their existence to a declining line of business . . . Having acquired some pretty little proficiency, they step before a public that has respect only for the highest technical achievement. . . . Presently the dream of gold and laurels will have been dreamed to a close, and those who had hoped to establish themselves on life's heights – we see them as obscure characters, going from house to house, inoculating younger generations with the virtuoso virus.

A superb pianist and a complete contrast to the Romantic peacocks was shy Adolf Henselt (1814–89) who must surely hold the record for practising. He devoted ten hours daily to it and even on journeys used a dummy keyboard resting on his knees. Unfortunately, despite his talent, he failed to achieve great fame owing to a lack of self-confidence and that made him shrink from playing in public. But, when at last he steeled himself to do so, the audience acclaimed him, and even Liszt was impressed. 'Find out the secret of Henselt's hands,' he advised his own pupils. 'I could have had velvet paws like that if I had wanted to.'

But becoming celebrated rendered Henselt more nervous. On one occasion he was eating quietly in a café when the band recognized him and cheered. Aghast, he jumped up, ran to the nearest exit and fled through the kitchen. It is not surprising therefore that in the whole of his life he gave only three concerts in public.

In 1830, Henselt became court pianist at St Petersburg, which suited him admirably because he played at matinées before small selected audiences, mainly of friends. Wilhelm von Lenz gives this vivid pen picture of him at home in the Russian capital:

Such a study of Bach as Henselt made, every day of his life, has never before been heard of. He played the fugues most diligently on a piano so muffled with feather quills that the only sound heard was the dry beat of the hammers against the muffled strings. It was like the bones of a skeleton rattled by the wind! In this manner, the great artist spared his ears and his nerves, for he reads, at the same time, on the music rack, a very thick, good book – the Bible – truly the most appropriate companion for Bach.

Pupils visiting Henselt for lessons would find him dressed in a white suit and a red fez, and clutching a fly-swatter. While they played, their teacher would walk around the room charging insects and exclaiming '*Falsch!* Play it again! *Falsch! Falsch!*' Should a pupil's lack of progress make him lose interest, he would put aside his fly-swatter, fetch in his dogs and play with them instead.

Anton Rubinstein (1830–94) was described at his peak as the 'most fiery, most fabulous, and most hypnotic' of pianists. It was said that when in the mood he would fret and fume and wish he had twenty pianos to play at the same time. Immensely popular in Britain, he visited the country first as a boy of twelve and then seven times between 1857 and 1886, and in the USA he toured widely to worshipping capacity audiences and contributed to its folklore. George W. Bagby created a backwoods character, called Jud Brownin, 'half chaw-bacon cutup, half lachrymose poet'. The following description, which became a recitation much in demand at parties for some 30 years in the States, tells how, according to the author, 'Jud Brownin Hears Ruby Play', some time in the 1870s:

Well, sir, he had the blamedest, biggest catty-corneredest pianner you ever laid your eyes on – something like a distracted billiard table on three legs. . . . When he first sit down, he peered to care mighty little about playing, and wished he hadn't come. He tweedle-eedled a little on the treble and twoodle-oodled some on the bass – just fooling and boxing the thing's jaws for being in his way. . . .

But presently his hands commenced chasing one another up and down the keys, like a passel of rats scampering through a garret very swift. Parts of it was sweet, though, and reminded me of a sugar squirrel turning the wheel of a candy cage. . . .

All of a sudden, old Ruby changed his tune. He ripped out and he rared, he pranced and he charged like grand entry at a circus. Peered to me that all the gaslights in the house was turned on at once, things got so bright, and I hilt up my head, ready to look any man in the face. It was a circus, and a brass band, and a big ball all going at the same time. . . . He set every living joint in me a-going . . . I jumped, sprang on to my seat and jest hollered – "Go it, my Rube!"

With that, some several policemen run up, and I had to simmer down. . . .

He had changed his tune again. He hop-light ladies and tiptoed fine from end to end of the keyboard. He played soft and low and solemn. I heard the church bells over the hills . . . then the music changed to water, full of feeling that couldn't be thought, and began to drop – drip, drop . . . falling into a lake of glory . . .

He stopped a moment or two to ketch breath. Then he got mad. He run his fingers through his hair, he shoved up his sleeve, he opened his coat tails a little further, he drug up his stock, he leaned over, and, sir, he jest went for that old pianner. He slapped her face . . . he pulled her nose, he pinched her ears, and he scratched her cheeks until she fairly yelled. She bellered like a bull, she bleated like a calf, she howled like a hound, she squeled like a pig, she shrieked like a rat . . . He ran a quarter stretch down the low grounds of the bass . . . through the hollows and caves of perdition. Then he fox-chased his right hand with his left till he got away out of the treble into the clouds, where the notes was finer than the points of cambric needles, and you couldn't hear nothing but the shadders of them.

By jinks, it was a mixtery! He fetched up his right wing, he fetched up his left wing, he fetched up his center, he fetched up his reserves. . . . He opened his cannon – round shot, shells, shrapnels, grape, canister, mines, and magazines – every living battery and bomb a-going at the same time. The house trembled, the lights danced, the walls shuck, the sky split, the ground rocked – heavens and earth, creation, sweet potatoes, Moses, ninepences, glory, tenpenny nails, Sampson in a 'simmon tree – Bang!!! . . .

With that bang! he lifted himself bodily into the air, and he came down with his knees, fingers, toes, elbows and his nose, striking every single solitary key on the pianner at the same time. . . . I knowed no more that evening.

Vladimir de Pachmann (1848–1933) was regarded at the height of his career as the finest interpreter of Chopin's music. One admirer thought that he had a tone like a rose leaf, whilst James Huneker, the American critic, called him the 'Chopinzee', an apt nickname in view of his appearance and antics. Pachmann refuted the charge that his pranks during recitals were motivated by a craving for front-page publicity and would assert that his patter and his grimacing were the channels through which he could give vent to his artistic feelings. Bernard Shaw called his affectations 'pantomimic performances with accompaniments by Chopin'.

Pachmann's London début was sensationally successful, and afterwards his riposte to a society lioness at a reception became the talk of the town. 'And what does Monsieur de Pachmann think of London?' she enquired.

'Zat iss not ze question, Madame,' he replied. 'Vat do London zink of de Pachmann? Zat iss ze question.'

Later, also in London, when playing his show piece, Chopin's

Minute Waltz, arranged in thirds, he bent low over the keyboard hiding his hands. 'Vy I do zis you vonder?' he explained. 'I vill tell. I see in ze owdience mein alte freund Moriz Rosenthal, and I do not vish him to copy my fingering.'

When the situation was reversed and it was Pachmann who was sitting with the public, other pianists would pale, dreading what he was likely to do. At a Godowsky concert, he suddenly jumped up and scrambled on to the platform. 'No, no, Leopold,' he shouted, pushing his rival off the stool and taking over. 'You must play it like so.'

Then having done this, he assured the spectators: 'Zat I vould not do for any one else. But Godowsky is ze zecond greatest liffing pianist.'

Pachmann's wife, Maggie Oakey, was also a pianist. He would attend her recitals, sometimes sitting concealed in the back row and encouraging her with cries of 'Charmant! Magnifique! Brava!'

Those invited to visit Pachmann would find him wearing a dirty old dressing-gown much too tight for his chubby figure, which he would proudly inform them had belonged to Chopin. 'It makes you cry, n'est-ce pas?' he told Harold Bauer, who relates how on an earlier occasion, when calling on Hans Richter at his home in Vienna, he had been received by him in a loose dressing-gown so ragged and dirty that Bauer was quite shocked. 'I notice your looks, young man,' said the conductor. 'Learn that this was Richard Wagner's.'

Before he commenced playing, Pachmann often made a tremendous fuss over getting the piano stool right for himself, struggling with its machinery, raising and lowering the height repeatedly. Then he would shake his head, stand thinking for a moment before hurrying offstage and, returning with a large ledger, put it on the stool. He would sit down, rise registering disgust, tear out a page and place that beneath him instead. Now, at last, a contented smile would spread over his features, and he would start playing. But rarely for long. Suddenly he would stop and ask his assembled admirers: 'Do you like ow I play?' Invariably they clapped and cheered. 'Den you are fools with no ears!' he would groan. 'I played like an elephant! Now I will play like only Pachmann can play!' Then, when he had finished and once more

113

they applauded, he would blow kisses at the piano and clap his hands at it.

Pachmann was popular with reporters because they always came away with entertaining stories. Once, in feigned fury, he shrieked: 'You zit zere when you should be on your knees before me.' On another occasion he assured a journalist that he dipped each finger in turn in cognac before a recital. In his 76th year, he told the press that his fingers were as nimble as ever through milking cows. A photograph of him on vacation in the Catskill Mountains with a pail over his arm, standing by a herd of them, appeared in American papers.

Moriz Rosenthal (1862–1946), from whom Pachmann jestingly hid his fingering, was probably Liszt's greatest pupil and the finest technician of his times. A critic described his tone as like that of a thunderbolt. He had a caustic wit. On learning that Artur Schnabel had been turned down for military service, he commented: 'Well, what did you expect? No fingers!' Once, when some pianists were signing a petition, the last one in the queue was annoyed to find hardly any space left. 'What am I supposed to write down here?' he demanded. 'Your repertoire,' suggested Rosenthal.

A friend, fond of playing Liszt's Sixth Rhapsody, took it too deliberately in Rosenthal's opinion. So, when this pianist made the excuse that he had been too busy to visit him, Moriz retorted: 'Nonsense! If you have time to play the Sixth Rhapsody like that, you could certainly spare time to come and see me.'

On another occasion, Rosenthal went to call on a pianist who was very ambitious to become established as a composer. Rosenthal noticed that the top of his colleague's piano was covered with scores of works by Richard Strauss, Wagner and others. Pointing at these, and assuming a naïve air, he exclaimed: 'What's all this? Good gracious, what a disappointment! And I had imagined that you composed by heart.'

Paderewski (1860–1941) was the most publicized and successful pianist since Liszt. After conquering Vienna, Paris and London, where he played on Erard pianos, he was approached in 1887 by the firm of Steinway which, worried by falling sales in the USA, was seeking the services of a brilliant pianist who, by playing on their instruments exclusively, would stimulate demand. Terms were agreed and a contract signed, then Paderewski made his début in New York in 1891. There followed a triumphant tour with 117 fully subscribed concerts. Paderewski was in his lifetime to harvest at least $10 million from the USA, where he would travel like royalty with his own railroad Pullman. This °contained a Steinway piano on which he would practise for hours during journeys. Accompanying him were his personal physician, masseur, chef, butler and tuner. He was also never without a small but vital piece of equipment in the form of a spirit lamp, for heating water in which he would dip his fingers for a minute or two to make them more supple before playing, as smaller towns had no hot water laid on in the halls. During the recitals the only illumination Paderewski would allow to be kept on was a solitary dim light, as distant as possible, for he claimed that artificial lighting upset his concentration.

Often, Paderewski gave encores lasting an hour and up to a thousand admirers would climb on to the stage to shake or kiss his hands (insured for $100,000) and beg for locks of his luxuriant golden red hair. Once, he received a letter from a leading socialite in the western United States paying fulsome compliments to his art, requesting 'a lock of hair' and enclosing a stamp for the postage. He told his secretary to send the following reply:

Dear Madam,

Mr Paderewski directs me to say that it affords him much pleasure to comply with your request. You fail to specify whose hair you desire, and, to avoid error, he has secured a sample from each of the staff en voyage, to wit, his manager, his secretary, his valet, his two cooks, and his waiter, together with a small portion from a cat and a mattress belonging to Mr Pullman, proprietor of the coach de luxe which we occupy. I have the honour to be your obedient servant . . . .

People waited patiently at the crossings for the train carrying him to pass. Candies and soap bore his name, and one of the best-selling toys for children was a model of a little man, wearing a black frock coat and a white bow tie, seated at a grand piano. When a screw was turned, his hands would fly up and down the keyboard and his extra large head would shake its fiery mane. Advertisers used the maestro's name to attract attention. One poster went:

115

PADEREWSKI IS THE KING OF PIANISTS
BUT
FINKELSTEIN IS THE EMPEROR OF DRY GOODS

When at last the lion of the keyboard would sail for Europe, weeping women would line the waterfront. A girl revealed she had three autographed photographs from Paderewski: 'One to frame and hang in my bedroom, one to paste inside the piano to improve its tone, and one to carry with me always.'

Modern music did not appeal to Paderewski, whose principal home, Riond Busson, was in the small Swiss town of Morges near Lausanne. One day at a reception given by Margot Asquith, she said to him: 'Living there you must know that dear friend of mine, Stravinsky. Don't you agree that he is the greatest composer?' This was hardly the most tactful of questions for not only was Paderewski's antipathy to such music well-known, but as an intensely patriotic Pole he did not particularly care for Russians. However, equal to the occasion, he answered: 'Monsieur Stravinsky and I used to bathe at the opposite end of the lake, so we never met in the water. And Morges being such a huge place we never met on land either.'

It was not long following this that, after Paderewski had given a recital in a theatre, a young admirer eager to get as near him as possible leapt from a box into the stalls shouting ecstatically: 'Mr Paderewski, you have sent me to heaven!' The pianist looked down and said gently: 'I am so glad to see that you have come back to earth.'

Half a century later Paderewski's business manager, Hugo Görlitz, disclosed that before concerts took place in New York he would give complimentary tickets to students, who agreed to rush wildly down the aisles on to the stage, cheering and gesticulating at a given signal, 'as though overcome with a mad desire to get a closer view of Paderewski performing his magic'. This went on till the outbreak of the Second World War when the fire department prohibited the practice.

But it must be said that he had a genuine following among the younger generation. The teenagers who nowadays idolize rock stars reacted similarly towards him. For example, the American newspaperman Alan Dale reported in 1899: 'There I was girled in.

A huge and dominant gynarchy seethed around me. There were girls in shirt waists of silk and of flannel; there were girls in loose corsets and in tight corsets. There were large and bouncing girls, and short and stubby ones. There were girls in hats and girls in bonnets. There were girls who wore wedding rings and girls who didn't . . .'

Harold Schonberg in *The Great Pianists* says of Paderewski: 'He was a man who hewed for himself by sheer force of will an improbable and fantastic career despite the fact that he had fewer pianistic gifts than many of his colleagues. He had style and a big heart, immense dignity, glamour, and produced golden sounds . . . And so while his competitors were counting his wrong notes, he was counting his dollars.'

Paderewski was also a great patriot and served Poland well. When he was Prime Minister, a financial crisis sent his country's currency tumbling and more and more paper money was being printed. The exigencies of office made him an hour late for a dinner engagement with Hugh Gibson, the American Minister in Warsaw. At last, when the great man arrived and they shook hands, the diplomat told him with a smile: 'Mr Prime Minister, we are here on American territory and, as you know, in America time is money.'

The other replied: 'My dear friend, don't you know that in my country time is only paper?'

Playing the Piano in a Blizzard

Artur Schnabel in 1945 gave some autobiographical talks to the students of the University of Chicago and described his experiences playing in English provincial concert halls. What he had found common to most of them was 'the artificial blizzard'. The audience, cocooned in thick woollens, were able to enjoy both the music and the invigoration of being out in the open air, but not so the performer.

Once, in a certain town, the icy blast trained on him was so strong, Schnabel alleged, that he thought the platform where he sat 'a death-trap'. He had warmed his fingers in the artists' room, but when he commenced playing, amid the potted palms trembling in the wind, his hands became increasingly cold until his fingers felt frozen stiff. He decided that not having 'the constitution of a Shetland pony' he would be unable to survive performing under such conditions a second time, so told his manager, Mr Tillett, that should the concert organizers ever suggest a return he must make some excuse such as that Mr Schnabel was nervous about his health.

However, five years later Tillett told the virtuoso that the hall in question had been renovated at great cost and was now extremely comfortable, and asked him if, in the circumstances, he would relent and accept an engagement. The pianist agreed. He was then on tour with the violinist Bronislav Hubermann giving joint sonata recitals; with them was a German tuner who was aware of Schnabel's dread of draughts. On their reaching the town, the tuner went ahead to the hall to attend to the piano, and when Schnabel arrived later, the other broke the bad news that gusts of cold air still swept the platform and that he had even located the hole in the wall through which it funnelled.

The hall itself had been superbly decorated and the carpet in the artists' room was luxuriously soft and deep, but some evil genie, disapproving of musicians, had succeeded in preserving un-diminished in strength the detested draughts on stage. On this occasion, a capacity audience overflowed on to the platform and there were people seated close to Schnabel, but still the breeze continued unchecked. On this occasion he was playing from music, which kept flapping about; this obliged the man turning the pages to hold his left arm over them, which made it difficult for the pianist to see the notes.

By the time Schnabel and Hubermann had begun the second item, Brahms's G major Sonata, they had abandoned any idea of playing *con amore*. Somewhere in the first movement, the former's part had been marked to indicate that the page-turner should go to the violin-stand and turn a page for Hubermann. Whilst this was being done, the pianist's music was blown to a place in the last movement, so he was forced to play from memory. Then the man returned and got in Schnabel's way trying to find the right page.

Those on the platform understood what had happened, and, at the close of the first movement, a girl rose and shyly presented Schnabel with a hairpin, saying: 'This perhaps might help.' The audience gave her an ovation, and as the page-turner seemed at a loss as to what to do with the pin Hubermann moved to the piano and showed him how to use it to clasp the pages together. They then continued the concert in somewhat better spirits.

After 1934, Schnabel said he would not play in Oxford again, where the hall used for concerts was above the police station on the third floor of an old building. His first recitals there had been on weekday afternoons and 'as it was winter' all the windows were open, so in addition to draughts there was the further disturbance of street noises. Then came the time when he played on a Saturday night in competition with roistering without and the phones ringing incessantly below in the police station.

Schnabel was about to commence on the second part of his programme when church bells rang, followed by chimes. He assumed it must be the clock starting to strike nine, so he waited, counting quietly. But the chimes, to his surprise, went on long after he had counted nine, and some members of the audience began to chuckle. This mystified him, and by the time he had reached seventy-five, he thought to himself that the chiming might go on for hours. So he began to play. No sooner had he done this than puppies in kennels on the other side of the cul-de-sac began barking furiously in opposition, and did not pause or falter until after he himself had ceased playing.

At least Schnabel was consoled with profuse apologies from those present. One explained: 'We should have told you about Great Tom of Christ Church, which strikes at nine o'clock to signal the closing of the college gates. It strikes 101 times because there were originally 101 students.' Someone else added: 'We ought to have chloroformed those puppies.'

On another occasion Schnabel visited a town on the coast in winter. His train arrived there two hours before the recital was due to commence at 5.00 pm, and as there were no taxi-cabs waiting at the station he strolled through the drizzle to the hall. The hall was built into a cliff, and he descended into it from the entrance above. To his astonishment, the place was already almost full with ladies. However, he soon discovered it was not enthusiasm for him that had brought them so early. They had come for afternoon tea and most were accompanied by their knitting.

A piano tuner was busy on the platform which, according to Schnabel, was well furnished with the sort of flowers one sees at funerals and of which he had never been fond. The noise from the tea being served and consumed was so loud that he asked the tuner to find out if it would continue during the concert. The man was told that it was expected to be all over by a quarter to five.

Schnabel then waited on a very hard chair in the artists' room, reached by a trap-door from the platform. The rain clouds blanketed the sea view through the only window. Not a soul appeared until ten to five when a man came down the steps, and said: 'I am the manager of this show. Glad to meet you. How long does your programme last?'

'Approximately two hours.'

'What a nuisance! What a nuisance! Well, you can take one piece out of the programme.'

'All right, I shall play one piece less, if you want.'

'Well, I am only the manager of this show. If the President comes, I shall suggest that to him. You know, our people have dinner at a certain hour and they would be very disturbed if this routine were changed. They are very orderly people, you know.'

Now they were joined by the President, a white-haired clergyman, whom the manager told firmly: 'Item number two won't be played by Mr Schnabel. Will you please announce that to the audience?' And, without asking why, the President returned to the platform and informed the gathering that Beethoven's Sonata Opus 110 would be omitted.

'Well, you can kick off at five o'clock sharp if you like,' the manager prompted Schnabel, who throughout his playing found the audience as lifeless and unresponsive as the funereal blooms about him. On account of the curtailed programme, he ended, it seemed, fourteen minutes before the listeners were accustomed to leave, which made the manager change his mind and declare: 'We want to get our money's worth. You can play thirteen more minutes!'

The virtuoso raised no objection and proceeded to practise some intermezzi by Brahms which he had to play a few days later elsewhere.

As his train to London was not due until after 8.00 pm, Schnabel did not hurry over changing in the artists' room and, when he climbed the ladder-like steps, it was to find all the lights extinguished in the building above. Fortunately he had a box of matches on him, but though he struck the lot he could not locate the exit, and was getting desperate when an electric torch shone through the blackness and he met a man who let him out, remarking: 'You're a lucky fellow. If I hadn't been here, you would have found yourself locked in all night.'

After walking back to the station through the rain, the weary pianist had time for a meal, but on enquiry was told: 'What a pity you weren't here for lunch. There's a very good place just opposite, but it's closed in the evening.'

Schnabel ended his discourse on the drawbacks of touring in Britain by claiming that when once he was performing in Glasgow, a dense fog penetrated through the open windows into the hall so that he actually could not see the audience. 'There *was* one, however.'

Child Prodigy

No branch of the arts has produced more child prodigies than that of music. In June, 1948, the popular press made much of the fact that over ten thousand people had packed the Harringay Arena to watch a boy of ten conduct. It was the largest known audience at an indoor concert in England in recent years, and yet earlier that year Sir Thomas Beecham had had to cancel a concert because only a hundred tickets had been subscribed. Commenting on this in the *Sunday Times*, Ernest Newman wrote: 'By all democratic standards, then (the counting of heads, regardless of what is inside them), this boy, who wore (and perhaps this is where Sir Thomas Beecham fell down) "black velvet with a white jabot and between each item hurried with his mother to his dressing-room to sip grapefruit juice", has saved our national credit.'

A boy conductor was, possibly, a novelty. The child prodigies of the past have played a musical instrument, usually the piano. Mendelssohn made his début at the age of nine; Chopin, who commenced at six, was rewarded for his brilliance during the following nine years – with a gold watch from the Queen of Song, Angelina Catalani, and a diamond ring from the Czar Alexander I; Liszt at thirteen was a sensation in London, where his landlady, instead of a laurel wreath, gave him an extra helping of his favourite English dish, gooseberry pie.

From time to time, *Punch* poked fun at these embryo virtuosi. For example, in 1888 a piece by F. Anstey described a Morning Concert by little Master Poushkin Poponanoff, 'the very latest, youngest, and smallest of Precocious Pianists'. The public besiege the box-office and the clerk repeats in response to frantic appeals: 'All the shilling seats are gone long ago.' But, surely, the disappointed applicants implore, there must be some standing room left? The man behind the grille relents. There are a few inches unoccupied at the back. Inside, there is trouble when a Strong-Minded Matron stands with her large family in the gangway between the five-shilling seats and refuses to move, telling the Polite Attendant (who then retreats, defeated): 'I am only a woman with these defenceless children, but I warn you that I will yield to nothing but superior force – you will have to drag us out!' Later, the wily woman, after the first interval, says to some male occupants of the stalls: '*Might* I ask you to allow my daughters to take your seats for a short time? They are quite unused to standing so long . . . Thank you so much!' The men then 'feeling a delicacy in reclaiming their seats, remain standing for the remainder of the performance'.

When Master Pushkin appears on the platform, he is received with tumultuous applause and an Enthusiastic Person, who has read a newspaper account of an interview with him, rhapsodizes to her neighbour: 'Isn't he sweet? Such perfect self-possession! See, he has to have a little pair of steps to climb on the music stool! Do you know he positively refuses to play a note unless they put one of his tin soldiers on the piano?'

A mother, desperate to reconcile her rebellious small son to piano lessons, tells him: 'Now, Jacky, you see what a little boy can do when he tries.' A governess points out to a Spectacled Schoolgirl: 'Just think, my dear Millie, how he must have *practised* to be able to play like this!' The girl shudders, anticipating what she will have to endure: 'It's too awful to think of!'

The Enth Person prefers Poushkin Poponanoff to all other child prodigies she has heard, for 'he's much *prettier*'. A Connoisseur assures his companion: 'I've heard that "Starlight Sonata" played by all the first pianists in Europe, and not one of them – not *one* – entered into the yearning discontent, the dreamy despair, the hopeless passion, with such feeling and perfect comprehension as this little Poushkin – a child of seven and a half. Sir – marvellous!'

As the second half is about to begin, the Enth Person gabbles: 'They say little Poushkin spends the intervals playing with his Noah's Ark and sucking sweets. Here he comes again! Look, his little cheek is quite bulged out. I shouldn't wonder if he had a bull's-eye in it. Isn't he a *duck*! Do you notice how he always sticks his legs out when he comes to the Scherzo?'

An Unappreciated Genius grumbles to his companion: 'So sickening, I call it, all this fuss about a kid! Why, I might play Mendelssohn and Chopin till I fell under the piano, and none of these people would give me a hand. *Would* they?' And the other replies: 'Well, not unless you could get yourself up in a frock and bows.'

A Humble Friend observes obsequiously to her Wealthy Patroness: 'Well, my dear, I always say just what I think, as you know, and I *do* say that your little Emmeline plays with quite as more *correctness* as this little Russian boy, and *far* more brilliancy of execution.'

The Wealthy Patroness, flattered, feels she must show her appreciation of the Humble Friend's discernment: 'So you really think so? Of course, she has been thoroughly well taught – and, now I think of it, if you've nothing to do tomorrow evening come in about ten – I can't ask you to dinner, because our table is full.'

A Proud Mother suggests to her bored husband: 'I've been thinking of such a charming plan if we can only manage it. I wonder if we could get little Poushkin to come to us one evening, and play that duet from *Zampa* with our little Josephine – she's *very* nearly perfect in it.'

The concert concludes with Master Poushkin's taking the lead in a trio with two full-grown performers as his foils. More recalls, general furore, subsiding, as the audience breaks up, into calmer criticism.

First Caviller: 'After all, you know, I think I prefer de Pachmann. This boy took the Allegro rather slow, I thought.'

Second Caviller: 'And it's so easy to substitute single notes for octaves. I don't call it legitimate, either, for *my* part.'

Then, a Professional recognizes an Ex-Phenomenon and inquires: 'And so you are no longer playing?'

Ex-Phenomenon: 'I am too big because – I can now stretch the octave.'

'They Laughed When
I Sat Down at the Piano'

The growing interest in learning to play musical instruments led to the founding of the Royal Academy of Music in 1822. This started as a school for children in Tenterden Street, London. William Gardiner in his *Music and Friends*, published in 1838, describes how he went there at a friend's request to see how a pupil was progressing.

Having rapped at the door, for the life of me I could not recollect the name of the boy. "Did he sing or play?" I was asked. I could not tell. I might take a peep into the different rooms, and see if I could find him.

In a large apartment were near twenty pupils, strumming upon as many piano-fortes, producing an instant jingle. In the singing-room they were sol-fa-ing in every kind of voice. Such a Babel I never wish to hear again. We then visited the violin department, the horrid scraping of which I could not endure. The horns were in a double closet, the oboes and flutes in the garret, and the trumpets in a cock-loft under the skylight. In a small out-office in the yard the drummer was at work, and near him the trombone was darting his instrument down a long entry. In returning I was mightily struck by a loud voice practising a shake up in a shower-bath. My youth I could not find, but, just as I was departing, the porter bethought himself of the fagotto, when lo! on opening a door, I beheld the object of my search on the cellar steps, pumping on his bassoon with all his might in the dark.

Famous pianists who took private pupils and wrote on the art of piano playing often gave conflicting advice. Anton Rubinstein's advice was simple. 'Walk – then your fingers will run.' Clementi wanted palm and hand to be still, with only fingers moving. Both he and Franz Hunten insisted that students should hold hands and arms in a horizontal position to the keys. Hummel and Bertini recommended playing with hands and wrists turned outward. Kalkbrenner sat to the right of the middle of the keyboard and played octaves with a loose wrist, but Moscheles considered the latter should be tight. Dussek sitting to the left of the middle favoured the left hand, and leant his hands towards the thumb. Liszt told Amy Fay: 'Keep your hand still, Fräulein, don't make an omelette.'

One would advocate that fingers should be held taut and stiff and another would insist on their being relaxed and loose; one said, 'Imagine your hand is a deadweight, then let it fall on to the keyboard'; another ordered: 'Forget you have a wrist and attack from the elbow.' There were those who wanted fingers to hit the ivories with sharp precision, like the legs of drilled soldiers on parade, and those who on the contrary would have fingers dance over the keys in a flowing, unbroken manner.

And to give a fillip to backward pupils some extraordinary machines were invented and marketed, the best-known being John Baptist Logier's Chiroplast. Made of brass and wood, it was clamped to the keyboard imprisoning the pupil's hands and wrists in the supposedly correct playing position. However, this obstructed the thumb, thus preventing the practising of scales. Then Friedrich Kalkbrenner brought out his modified version of the Chiroplast, the '*guide-mains*', which held the arms firmly horizontal to the keyboard. Next came Henri Herz's 'Dactylion', consisting of a set of vertical springs, to be hung upright over the keyboard. A wire dangling from each carried a ring at its end, and the player was expected to put each finger through one of these, stretching the spring as he did so. The strain of the spring was meant to encourage the swift lift of the finger when released, thus making for a clear articulation. A book of no fewer than a thousand exercises was supplied.

Fifty years later in the 1880s, when the 'Dactylion' had been forgotten, Theodore Presser revived it in America. As shown in contemporary advertisements it looks like a medieval instrument of torture, gripping the wrist in a vice and the fingers in thumbscrews.

The longing among the piano-obsessed to play like a virtuoso was so strong that the inventors of these contrivances had no difficulty in selling them. F.L. Becker, a piano teacher in New

York, offered his 'Manumoneon' for $10; users could perform, with the aid of its 'gymnastic appliances', exercises to develop technique. Another New Yorker, C.H. Bidwell, sold for a third of the price of the Manumoneon a 'Pocket Hand Exerciser', supported from the floor by a foot stirrup, that would 'prepare the hands for the keyboard'.

The wealthy might have fancied J. Brotherhood's 'Technicon', costing $22.50 in walnut, $27.00 in mahogany. To attract the lazy, this impressive assembly of levers, counter-weights, rollers, etc., had elbow rests. By manipulating it in accordance with the instructions, costing 75 cents, the lifting and pushing power of all the muscles of the hand could be strengthened.

Sir Eugene Goossens relates how in 1929 he visited Stravinsky in his Paris studio and found him practising the piano vigorously with the aid of some iron dumbbells which, every now and then, he would raise over his head and then slowly put down again on the floor.

'What are you using them for?' Goossens asked.

'For the development of the forearm,' Stravinsky replied. 'I find this additional muscular strength very helpful in playing my music.'

Apart from all these devices for encouraging keyboard athleticism, there was another way those desperate to do so could learn to startle their friends with their piano-playing. The following advertisement, the brain-child of the then 25-year-old John Capler, was so successful in attracting customers that he became one of the most sought-after advertising copywriters of his day.

The advertisement was headed:

'THEY LAUGHED WHEN I SAT DOWN AT THE PIANO BUT WHEN I STARTED TO PLAY!'

The rest read:

Arthur had just played "The Rosary". The room rang with applause. I decided that this would be a dramatic moment for me to make my début. To the amazement of all my friends I strode confidently over to the piano and sat down.

"Jack is up to his old tricks," somebody chuckled. The crowd laughed. They were all certain that I couldn't play a single note.

127

"Can he really play?" I heard a girl whisper to Arthur. "Heavens, no!" Arthur exclaimed. "He never played a note in all his life. But just you watch him. This is going to be good."

I decided to make the most of the situation. With mock dignity, I drew out a silk handkerchief and lightly dusted off the keys. Then I rose and gave the revolving piano stool a quarter of a turn, just as I had seen an imitator of Paderewski do in a vaudeville sketch.

"What do you think of his execution?" called a voice from the rear.

"We're in favor of it!" came back the answer, and the crowd rocked with laughter.

Instantly, a tense silence fell on the guests. The laughter died on their lips as if by magic. I played through the first bars of Liszt's immortal Liebesträume. I heard gasps of amazement. My friends sat breathless – spellbound . . .

As the last notes died away, the room resounded with a sudden roar of applause . . . How my friends carried on! . . . Everyone was exclaiming with delight – plying me with rapid questions . . . "Where *did* you learn?" – "How long have you studied?" – "Who was your teacher?"

"I have never *seen* my teacher," I replied. "And just a short while ago, I couldn't play a note."

"Quit your kidding," laughed Arthur, himself an accomplished pianist. "You've been studying for years. I can tell."

"I have been studying only a short while," I insisted. "I decided to keep it a secret, so that I could surprise all you folks."

Then I told them the whole story.

"Have you ever heard of the U.S. School of Music?" I asked. A few of my friends nodded. "That's a correspondence school, isn't it?" they exclaimed.

"Exactly," I replied. "They have a new simplified method that can teach you to play any instrument by rote in just a few months – only costs a few cents a day . . . You, too, can now teach yourself to be an accomplished musician – right at home in half the usual time. You can't go wrong with this simple new method which has already shown almost half a million people how to play their favorite instrument *by rote*. Forget that old-fashioned idea that you need special talent . . ."

Piano War

Even in Victorian times, the praise of experts and those in the public eye was being exploited commercially to attract sales. The achievements of the titans of the keyboard aroused a yearning among the musically-minded to emulate them and it was not difficult to persuade people that a short-cut to success would be to use the same kind of piano. Hell, wrote a cynic, is a piano warehouse where pianists galore play for ever such pieces as 'The Maiden's Prayer'.

The sales of Steinway grands increased in the 1880s thanks to two letters reproduced in the firm's illustrated sales brochure stating that during the first Bayreuth Festival of 1876 a number of new grands 'of the most celebrated European as well as of several American makers had been placed at Mr Richard Wagner's disposal; among them a new Centennial Concert Grand piano made by Steinway & Sons of New York, which, from its wonderful power, beauty, and sympathetic quality of tone, far outshone all rival instruments, and which Mr Richard Wagner at once chose for his own private use.'

But this was only the opening gambit. Early in 1879, we are told, Mr Wagner was requested by Mr Thomas Steinway to send this grand piano to the Steinway Central European Depot to be fitted with the latest invention, The 'Tone Pulsator', patented in July, 1878. The composer complied and then, only a few weeks later, on 11 March 1879, wrote from Bayreuth:

My dear Mr Steinway,

                I miss my Steinway Grand, as one misses a beloved wife; it is wanting everywhere. I no longer indulge in music since

129

that Grand is gone, and trust its absence will not be too long protracted.

Very truly yours,
Richard Wagner.

The speed with which the grand piano, now fitted with its 'Tone Pulsator', was returned to its owner is certainly an object lesson for today's manufacturers. The following month, on 11 April, the composer sent a fulsome and lengthy testimonial:

My dear Mr Steinway,

Really you ought personally to have witnessed the gratification which I experienced upon receiving back your magnificent Grand piano; you certainly would not have asked me to add another word. . . .

I know of nothing in painting, sculpture, architecture, literature, and, unfortunately, also music, which – since I have comprehension of the same – could compare with the masterly perfection reached in piano-forte building. . . .

A Beethoven Sonata, a Bach Chromatic Fantasia, can only be fully appreciated when rendered upon one of your piano-fortes.

The next sentence should have been of distinct encouragement to the average amateur:

Although I do not possess the slightest dexterity in piano-forte playing, I delight in being able to do justice to your assumption of my inborn and cultivated sense of tone. For sounds of such beauty as those coming from my Steinway Grand flatter and coax the most agreeable tone-pictures from my harmonic melodic senses.

IN A WORD, I FIND YOUR GRAND PIANO OF WONDROUS BEAUTY. IT IS A NOBLE WORK OF ART. And with a thousand thanks for this new attention, I delight in being able to call myself your friend,

Richard Wagner.

The Steinway catalogue also contained shorter letters of praise from such celebrities as Franz Liszt, Adelina Patti and Anton Rubinstein. Proudly, Steinway announced in its advertisements: 'One piano every working hour! Ten pianos a day!'

Steinway seems to have been successful in weaning Wagner away from the Bechstein company, but this did not prevent the latter in its catalogue dated March, 1892 from continuing to print a letter from the composer dated 25 May 1864, that reads:

My dear Mr Bechstein,

Three years ago, when for the first time I returned to Germany from my exile, I stayed with my friend Liszt in Weimar, and there by chance I came across a pianoforte which, by its sparkling yet deliciously sympathetic tone, gave me such delight and so entranced me that when, at our sad parting, my dear Hans von Bülow entreated me to tell him what he could do for me to cheer me in my sadness, the animating idea sprang to my mind that he should procure for me, at the place where I should at length find my home, such an instrument as this. . . . And now that I have found my last, long-sought-for home, it is you who brighten it and assist me in my work by this magnificent and noble instrument. Thus has my long-cherished wish received a grand fulfilment!

Testimonials were also included from Liszt and Rubinstein, both of whom had written in similar terms to Steinway. Bechstein's catalogue also shows the company to have been suppliers to Queen Victoria and her family, most of the crowned heads of Europe, innumerable princes and princesses, grand dukes and duchesses, and leading conservatoires. It goes on: 'The Bechstein Factories are already of colossal magnitude, but vast extensions, necessitated by the ever-increasing demand, are in progress.'

Steinway, six months earlier, had already staked its claim to being ahead in the 'snob' stakes. In the *Musical Courier* for 14 October 1891 in a double-page advertisement on special glazed paper in purple and gold, Steinway boasted that it, too, was a purveyor of pianos to Queen Victoria and the Prince and Princess of Wales, as well as to 174 patrons – 'almost all belonging to British or English-resident foreign nobility'. There followed the names of five dukes and duchesses, nine marquesses and marchionesses, 27 earls and countesses, ending with thirteen 'Honourables' plus ten generals, admirals and colonels. After this list to impress lesser beings, the latter were advised: 'You, too, can be a duke – well, not quite, really. But you can acquire a tinge of the celebrated dukishness by buying the same brand of piano as did

His Grace. Then you can use its keyboard to play, "Nearer, My Lord to Thee." '

The tradition continues, for in *Music – A Joy for Life*, Edward Heath proudly pointed out that his Steinway was the first pianoforte to be moved into 10 Downing Street since Arthur Balfour resigned in 1905.

In 1878 Steinway had faced fierce competition from other piano manufacturers in the USA, so when Mapleson presented a season of opera that October at the Academy of Music, New York, they offered to supply the principal singers with pianos both for use at the theatre and at their hotels. The offer was accepted, and later a letter, dated 28 December and signed by Etelka Gerster, Marie Roze, Minnie Hauk, Clarice Sinico, Italo Campanini and others, expressed the singers' 'unqualified admiration' of these pianos' 'sonority, evenness, richness, astonishing durability of tone, most beautifully blending with and supporting the voice'. These 'matchless qualities' made them 'the most desirable instruments for the public generally'.

When the company reached Philadelphia the following February, they found magnificent Steinways already installed in their bedrooms. The widely-publicized testimonial had increased that firm's sales to the detriment in particular of the house of Weber. So Albert Weber himself organized a counter-coup, and, whilst the singers were dining, his men invaded the bedrooms, put all the Steinways out in the passage and substituted Weber's showpieces.

On learning what had happened, Steinways sent their men to the hotel to eject the rival pianos and replace their own. Having suspected that this might happen, the Weber squad were lying in wait and a pitched battle broke out in the corridor with piano legs, unscrewed from their cases, being used as weapons. Victory went to the Weber side, and that night Adolphe Weber held a grand celebratory supper for the whole company – all of whom, to Mapleson's astonished amusement, and after enjoying the best of champagne, signed a paper to the effect that Weber's pianos were the finest they had ever known.

Mapleson adds in his memoirs that 'such was the impartiality of my singers' that they not long afterwards signed a testimonial for yet another pianoforte manufacturer, Haines and Co.

During the Chicago World's Fair of 1893, Steinway did not

exhibit its range of pianos. Theodore Thomas, then the most prominent American conductor, had arranged with Paderewski to take part in a concert there. Paderewski would play only Steinways. Then, just four days before the event, a Congressional Commission passed a resolution that no piano should be used in the Exposition grounds except those represented by firms exhibiting at the Fair. They also gave instructions that if any Steinway pianos were brought into the grounds for intended use at the concerts, the Director General was 'to send teams and dump the pianos outside the gates'. Further still, 'the bills announcing Mr Paderewski's appearance with the Exposition Orchestra must be taken down and Mr Paderewski's name erased'.

However, Thomas decided to ignore the Commission's orders and the Exposition's directors looked the other way when a Steinway was smuggled in. Paderewski played his own concerto on this instrument, supported by the Exposition Orchestra. No one appeared to remove it and the occasion was a tremendous success. The critics of the *Chicago Herald* and *Evening Post*, nevertheless, attacked Paderewski, claiming that he had treated the USA and the Commission with contempt by playing the work of 'greasy foreigners such as Chopin and Schumann instead of honest American music'.

At least Paderewski had performed on a piano made in the USA. Another well-established firm of American manufacturers was that founded by Jonas Chickering in Boston. It was his adventurous son Frank who shipped one of their grands to Europe, transporting it through the Alps to Liszt in Rome. There the maestro, after playing it, exclaimed: 'I never thought a piano could have such qualities.' When Liszt's son-in-law Hans von Bülow toured the USA, the Chickerings persuaded him to perform only on their instruments. He made his début on 18 November 1875 in Boston's new concert hall and capacity audiences attended the first four concerts. Bülow, however, was arrogant and irascible and some derisive remarks he made about gross, beer-swilling American Germans of low musical tastes were reported in the New York *Sun* which made him very unpopular. In Baltimore, during a rehearsal, he noticed that a board with the name 'CHICKERING' in huge gilt capitals was attached to the side of the piano facing the auditorium. He tore it off and threw it angrily on to the platform shouting, 'I am not a travelling advertisement'. Later he tied it to the tail end of the piano and sat kicking it. Eventually, the tour ended prematurely owing to his unpopularity.

In the battle to keep ahead of competitors, piano manufacturers were continually seeking ways of improving their instruments. In the second quarter of the nineteenth century, 1098 patents were taken out, chiefly in England and France. The word 'patent' itself was so plugged in advertisements that it came to suggest to the more gullible members of the public almost magical additional qualities. For those who suffered from unmusical complaining neighbours Behr Brothers provided a 'Patent Piano Muffler', whilst Lonover Brothers enticed customers with a 'Patent Repeating Action Metallic Rail', a 'Patent Duplex Bridge with Auxiliary Vibrators', a 'Patent Telescope Lamp Bracket', and a 'Patent Automatic Music Desk'.

But the palm for a plethora of patents must surely be awarded to Paul G. Mehlin and Sons, boasting of nine – for a Grand Plate and Scale, a Touch Regulator, a Grand Fall Board, a Harmonic Scale, an Endwood Bridge, a Finger Guard, a Steel Action Frame, a Cylinder Top and Tone Reflector, and (as a counter-blow to Behr Brothers) an improved Piano Muffler.

Much interest was shown by visitors to the Great Exhibition of 1851 in a 'Patent Bed' with a pianoforte which the lazy could cause to play a soothing repertoire by lying on it. Then, fifteen years later, an attempt was made to cater for pianists whose families objected to their playing in the only sitting-room, even on an instrument fitted with a patent muffler, when Millward were granted a patent for an all-purpose instrument that could be accommodated in a bedroom. Tucked away in its inside would be a couch on rollers, a bureau, and two closets – one for storing bed clothes and the other containing a wash-basin, jug, towels and 'other articles of toilet'.

For the nautical musician, William Jenkins and Son of London produced an 'expanding and collapsing piano for gentlemen's yachts, the saloons of steam-vessels, ladies' cabins, etc., only 13½ ins. from front to back when collapsed', whilst for those who wanted a piano principally as a prestige decoration rather than for use, George H. Aggio of Colchester could supply one 'fitted up in a plate glass case, and gold carvings with an embroidered curtain front'. There was one boon to playing that all pianists would have welcomed but inventors failed to find – some foolproof gadget for turning pages.

In America, the *Musical Courier* had originally been the *Musical and Sewing Machine Gazette* because in Victorian times the same commercial travellers sold both the latter and pianos, and not because any ingenious mind had produced a hybrid version of the two. Lesser-known manufacturers supplied pianos giving no indication of their origin, which enabled dealers to add by means of transfers or stencils either their own names or any other they might care to invent. Sidney Harrison, the distinguished pianist, relates how he met in Canada a dealer who told him he had sold Japanese pianos as made by Steigermann, a name he had concocted by taking the syllable Stein from Steinway, removing the final letter and putting it at the end of the word 'German'.

In due course, testimonials from royalty and celebrities began to lose their selling value, especially when, as in the instances already mentioned, potential customers found the same people praising rival pianos. As sales promotion became more deft, other tactics were employed. My favourite piano advertisement appeared in San Francisco, and it quoted a mouse as saying:

One night I had been ousted from a warm nest where my wife and myself proposed to stay all the winter, by a hard-headed servant girl. . . . Oddly enough we had to remove to the drawing-room, a place barren of food. . . . A home we had to have and my wife, who was always musically inclined, proposed the piano. . . . As she insisted, I volunteered to gnaw a hole through it, but I found it tough work, as the independent iron frame and solid wood resisted my efforts. . . . The gas had been left burning . . . cautiously I surveyed the premises, when my dazzled vision gradually read the magic word STECK. I told my waiting wife that sacrilege was not included in my list of crimes and we wintered in an adroitly made nest in a velvet lounge. . . . We never repented our virtuous decision, for night after night we were lulled to sleep by its dulcet sound, its perfect tone, and the very soul of music which seemed to dwell in its touch.

Audiences

Had anyone murdered Arnold Bennett, top of the list of suspects might well have been a music buff who had read *Things That Have Interested Me*, in which the novelist wrote: 'Why are the frequenters of serious concerts so alarmingly ugly? And why do their features usually denote harsh intellectuality and repudiation? Why have they the air of mummies who have crept out of the Pyramids in order to accomplish a rite? Why have they not the air of having come into a public-house to get a pint of beer?'

Fritz Kreisler clearly did not find the state of blissful stillness into which his brilliant playing sent audiences a pretty sight. Once when the virtuoso violinist was out strolling with a friend in New York they happened to pass a fishmonger's shop. He pointed at the rows of gaping mouths and protruding eyes on the slab and remarked: 'I almost forgot – I have a concert tonight.'

Josef Hoffmann was reminded of another kind of food when, in February, 1920, the first of a series of Sunday afternoon concerts was given by the New Symphony Orchestra in the Royal Albert Hall. The depressingly small audience was apathetic but Hoffmann playing the Rubinstein concerto succeeded in stirring it from its Sunday stupor and he told the conductor, Eugene Goossens, afterwards: 'They sleep after their roast beef.'

'The next time you go to a concert, look around,' wrote Alfred Bendiner in *Music To My Eyes*, referring to American audiences.

All those who are not asleep are looking intently forward into the blinding light which covers the face of an orchestra; I am sure that most of them are thinking about whether they left the front door unlocked or the gin bottle uncorked. I doubt if anybody in the audience can sit through a whole concert and listen to every note and enjoy it thoroughly. The people who enjoy a whole concert and listen to every note are the members of the orchestra themselves.

Of course, not all concert-goers are necessarily music-lovers. They may be there because it is the fashionable thing to do. Sir Georg Solti, when conductor of the Chicago Symphony, was outspoken about the dreariness and inattentiveness of 'subscription' audiences, especially the Friday afternoon dowager crowd. 'I don't believe in one sex,' he commented.

Perhaps the trouble with such audiences is that they have too much of a good thing. A woman moved from her very small home-town to Chicago, happy that her dream of hearing fine music brilliantly played would at last be realized. So she went to a Chicago Symphony concert, and during the interval she talked to the lady who sat next to her, expressing her delight. The other, who had lived all her life in Chicago, replied: 'Well, I am a subscriber, this is my twenty-fifth season. I don't even listen any more.'

Music has proved a growth industry in the USA. Some twenty years ago, at a White House concert held on 16 August 1962, the late President John F. Kennedy said: 'Last year, more Americans went to symphonies than to baseball games. This may be viewed as an alarming statistic, but I think that both baseball and the country will survive.' It has been said that the dream of many a gigolo was that some rich doll would start up and endow an orchestra and instal him as conductor.

In Europe, festivals have proliferated. Never one to mind his words, Sir Thomas Beecham has said: 'All festivals are bunk. They are for the purpose of attracting trade to the town. What that has to do with music, I don't know.'

Others frequent concerts or the opera out of a sense of duty because they are relatives or friends of players or singers. The fiancée of a young violinist paid her first visit to the opera to hear him play in the orchestra for a performance of *Così fan tutti*. Afterwards, she told him: 'Oh, I liked it, dear. The costumes were heavenly! But couldn't they have got some other music for it?'

There are times when audiences applaud for reasons other than appreciation of the music. In an article headed 'The Tyranny of the Audience' that appeared in the *Musical Courier* for 1 April 1925,

William Weaver suggested there might be a touch of malice in what an artist could be misled into considering a compliment, as in the case of a young woman pianist playing a concerto at a minor concert. She arrived wearing an extremely tight new skirt which impeded her movements as she struggled on to the platform. After climbing up a step and walking past the first violinist, she was faced with the tricky task of negotiating a steeper step to the piano and almost plunged head first into its interior. When her performance was over, she had even greater difficulty in leaving the platform. She was recalled four times, not because of her playing but because of the fun provided by that tight skirt.

All artists suffer at times from the bad manners of audiences, such as arriving late and noisily. Leopold Stokowski once decided to teach those responsible a lesson. Instead of starting a symphony concert at the advertised time, he arranged for the players to lounge about the stage and its vicinity chatting and joking with one another for a good ten minutes before they settled down and he mounted the podium. He did not have to repeat the lesson. At the next concert the whole audience arrived early and behaved perfectly.

Stokowski employed somewhat similar tactics to cure the elderly ladies attending the Friday matinées at Philadelphia of their coughing, and he even succeeded in interesting them in some modern music. After his orchestra had performed Ravel's *Bolero* there for the first time, he happened to be walking home when he saw a dowager he knew slightly being helped into her Cadillac. 'Oh, maestro!' she called. 'Please do play again that divine *Bordello* next week.' Later, he asked a friend how the woman could have known a word like 'bordello' – which he didn't even know himself at that time.

Then there is the man who accompanies his girl-friend to an opera or a concert because she dotes on it, and who, becoming bored, talks to her, much to the annoyance of those around. This once happened to an acquaintance of mine. Seated behind a talkative nuisance, he at last exclaimed in exasperation: 'What a pest!' The culprit turned round and uttered indignantly, 'Did you refer to me, sir?'

'Oh, no!' was the response. 'I meant those musicians who are making such a row with their gear I can't hear what you're saying.'

Oscar Wilde, had he been present, might have riposted: 'If one hears bad music, it is one's duty to drown it by one's conversation' (*The Portrait of Dorian Gray*), or 'Musical people are so absurdly unreasonable. They always want one to be perfectly dumb at the very moment when one is longing to be absolutely deaf', or 'If one plays good music, people don't listen, and, if one plays bad music, people don't talk' (*The Importance of Being Earnest*), or, perhaps most crushingly of all: 'I like Wagner's music better than anybody's. It's so loud that one can talk the whole time without other people's hearing what one says' (*The Portrait of Dorian Gray*).

Of course, there is a risk that verbal exchanges might have unpleasant consequences. Norman Tucker relates how, when he went with a singer friend to hear *Lohengrin* at the old Streatham Hill Theatre, soon after the curtain rose a lady seated two rows ahead in the circle started explaining the plot to her husband. After politely but ineffectually requesting quiet several times, the friend, exasperated beyond endurance, leant forward, repeated his demand and rapped the offender smartly on the head with a vocal score. Peace reigned thereafter.

Sir Thomas Beecham expressed his views on audiences at various times. 'I never conduct above an audience's head – it is an impertinence to do so for it has paid to be pleased,' he told an interviewer. 'The grand tune is the only thing the public understands, and flexibility is the only thing that makes music appeal.' He really did not have too high an opinion of the customers, as may be gathered from these remarks to his orchestra:

There are only two things to remember – you begin together – and you end together. What you do in between doesn't matter. The audience won't know, anyway. That is the Golden Rule.

If you are satisfied that what you are doing at the moment is right – even if it is wrong that is all that matters. Whether you are singing or conducting – or misconducting – do it with conviction. And remember the English may not like music – but they absolutely love the noise it makes.

Sir Thomas's disdain included even the musically knowledgeable. At the 1959 Lucerne Festival he conducted the Philharmonia

Choir and Orchestra in a version of the *Messiah* which he had commissioned from Sir Eugene Goossens. In his biography of Beecham, Charles Reid gives his impression after attending a general rehearsal: 'As rescored by Goossens Handel's music glowed, boomed and tinkled unprecedentedly. The brass and percussion writing often smacked of Elgar and *Die Meistersinger*, with tinctures here and there of Rimsky-Korsakov.'

'What are the purists going to say about all this?' Reid enquired.

'My dear boy,' Beecham answered, 'I never think about the purists. They are a breed that has sprung up recently. If Handel and many other composers were left to the purists, with their parsimonious handfuls of strings and oboes, you would never hear any of them. The thing to remember is that no man knows how these works were performed originally. . . . Handel, who played the organ, clavichord and harpsichord in these performances, was the greatest *improvisatore* of his day. Anybody who had the good fortune as I had to hear the improvisations of the greatest cathedral organists of the nineteenth century knows what extraordinary things the *improvisatore* can do in "filling-in". There is no such filling-in by our purists. I have done purist versions of the *Messiah* myself all over the world. Invariably the public walk out.'

Probably the most musically-ignorant in Beecham's audiences were those who supported him generously with money, such as Emerald, Lady Cunard, When a section of his orchestra was performing in her drawing-room for a party, she was heard shouting to him, 'Sir Thomas, when are you going to play that lovely piece of Delius that you were rehearsing this afternoon?'

He smiled indulgently and replied, 'We have just this moment played it, my dear.'

Gerald Moore in *Am I Too Loud?* tells how in the same room he saw Lady Cunard seize Ida Haendal's Stradivarius by the strings and swing it in the air asking why it was so precious. It was a *nouveau riche* hostess living not far from Lady Cunard who, on being told by the leader of a newly-formed string quartet that they were in great demand, exclaimed: 'How splendid! Now you're making money you'll be able to afford to add to your numbers.'

The audiences that Sir Thomas Beecham would take particular pains over pleasing were those of children. Neville Cardus has written that one of his most affectionate remembrances of

Beecham was his appearance, during his last years, at a Sir Robert Mayer Children's Concert. He began 'with an adorable touch' comments Cardus. 'Ladies and gentlemen,' the great man told the children, 'my slow progress to the conductor's desk was due not to any reluctance on my part to conduct before so distinguished an audience. My slow progress was due to the infirmity of old age.' A pause, then: 'And now, ladies and gentlemen, our first piece is by Mozart. It was composed when he was at the age of – er at the age of . . .' He pointed to a small boy in the front row. 'At your age, sir.'

The wealthy members of society who have patronized musicians have rarely done it because they understood and loved music. In the days when minor royalties abounded in Europe, it was a matter of prestige to employ a private orchestra. Ludwig Spohr at the commencement of his career was engaged as a violinist in the Duke of Brunswick's. The court concerts in the apartments of the Duchess, held once a week, were thoroughly disliked by the musicians as card parties took place at the same time. The Duchess therefore ordered the orchestra to play softly and also had a thick carpet laid on the floor under them. As a result one heard the words 'I bid', 'I pass', etc., much more loudly than the deadened music.

In Victorian times, musicians were paid to perform at London social gatherings where the guests were wont to chatter to each other the whole while the programme was in progress. It mattered little or nothing who the artists were. William Kuhé tells in *My Musical Recollections* how he agreed to play at a crowded 'at home' the day before he was to première a piece at a concert in the Hanover Square Rooms, so the idea occurred to him to take advantage of this opportunity to rehearse it in advance of the morrow. So he did this to the accompaniment of the usual babel, which sometimes made it difficult for him to hear the notes he struck. He comments that it was probably on this account that he was rewarded with considerable plaudits on rising from the piano.

When his turn came to play again, he repeated the composition, knowing full well that in the din of never-flagging conversation, the chances were ten to one against anyone noticing the repetition. He was proved right, for so high-pitched were the voices of the 'listeners' and so incessant was their prattle that, as he puts it, 'it would have made no difference whether I played the Dead March from *Saul* or "Tommy Make Room For Your Uncle".'

Yet a third time was he asked to give the guests an opportunity of exercising their conversational powers to the accompaniment of his playing and he readily complied – 'but I stuck to the piece in the rendering of which I hoped to surpass myself at the next day's concert'.

The result was the same. 'Talk, laughter, final crash on the iron-grand, followed by prolonged applause, mingled with cries of "Charming!" – "Quite exquisite!" – etc.' Wilhelm Kuhé's hostess, in particular, was lavish in the compliments she bestowed on him, saying he had given her friends 'a great artistic treat'. Then it was that Kuhé asked her which of the three pieces he had played she liked the best.

'Well,' she replied, after duly considering the point. 'I think I preferred the second one. Not that I didn't appreciate the others, only the second was so sweetly melodious.'

Kuhé ends: 'I told her I thought her discrimination wonderful. And so it was.'

Artur Schnabel in *My Life and Music* concluded that audiences in general were very good and unjustly blamed, again and again, for faults made by artists or managers. When asked after giving a pianoforte recital: 'What do you think of our audience?' his reply, he says, was: 'I know two kinds of audiences only – one coughing and one not coughing.' Such an answer he knew disappointed people for they wanted him to say: 'I have never had an audience like the one in your city.' But however much Schnabel might approve of his audience, his rule was to refuse to play encores, because, he explained: 'Applause is a receipt, not a bill.'

Bursting the Vanity Balloon

'To what base uses we may return, Horatio!' cried Hamlet. 'Why may not imagination trace the noble dust of Alexander, till he find it stopping a bung-hole?' The very manuscripts of writers and composers have suffered similar fates. Artur Schnabel wrote in *My Life and Music*: 'I heard stories in Vienna (I am sure they are true) that grocers were wrapping up cheese in Schubert mss. That reminds me that the manuscript of Bach's Six Brandenburg Concertos was sold, from a cart, for little more than a shilling, but that was not in Vienna.'

Bearing in mind, therefore, how transient are all forms of fame, those accustomed to public adulation in their lifetime need to be philosophical on finding their pride given unexpected knocks. Regularly after virtuoso Mischa Elman had given a concert, a boy would appear demanding his autograph. At last, the violinist asked: 'Why are you collecting so many?' Cheekily, the lad explained: 'Oh, I'm trading my pal five Elmans for one Kreisler.' Elman laughed and often repeated this story against himself.

Kreisler, too, had a similar experience. He was lunching at the Ritz on Boston when two very respectable-looking ladies stopped at his table. 'You have given us so much happiness,' the eldest said, 'that we could not resist the impulse of requesting you to autograph this menu for us.'

'Yes,' added the other, 'my sister and I were just saying our admiration goes back to 1924 when they first came out – and do you know we've never since driven anything else but one of your cars!'

Kreisler smiled but made no comment as he wrote on the menu: 'With the appreciation and best wishes of Walter P. Chrysler.'

When in Zurich, Otto Klemperer went into what was reputed to be the best stocked music shop to buy a copy of one of his own records as a gift for a friend. George Mendelssohn-Bartholdy of the Vox company accompanied the eminent German conductor, who asked at the counter: 'Have you the recording of Beethoven's *Eroica* Symphony conducted by Klemperer?'

The salesman went away and searched through the stock, then he returned and said: 'I'm afraid we haven't, but we have recordings of the *Eroica* by Furtwängler, Bruno Walter, Koussevitzky . . .'

'*Nein, nein*, it must be Klemperer. Have another look.'

The young man complied, but, after a time returned, shaking his head. 'I've hunted everywhere. We have other recordings by Klemperer, but not Beethoven's *Eroica*. However, I can recommend the Furtwängler.'

'You don't understand,' snapped the frustrated customer. 'You see, I am Klemperer.'

'Oh, yes?' responded the salesman, disbelievingly. 'And I suppose this other gentleman is Beethoven?'

'*Nein, nein!*' retorted Klemperer truthfully. 'He's Mendelssohn.'

'*I think the Beecham recording is still the best.*'

The Power of Music

Music is not only the food of love but also probably the most powerful force in the world. According to the Old Testament, the walls of Jericho were demolished by the sound of trumpets, and it is said that by playing a church's key note for too long a time on an organ the whole edifice could be brought down. Caruso shattered a wine glass in this fashion, and stories have been told about sopranos doing the same with their high notes to opera glasses, mirrors in the foyer, bottles in the bars, and even windscreens out in the car park. The music of the composer Jacques Halévy had a more blasting effect once. It did not satisfy him to mark passages 'f' and 'ff', so he would attempt to increase the decibel power of orchestras with markings of up to six 'f's. It is said that one evening when he himself was conducting a brass band, Halévy so roused the players that the French horn was blown quite straight.

Scientists, too, have reached some interesting conclusions. Two hundred years or so ago Ernst Chladni, the German physicist, placed a thin metal plate on a violin, sprinkled sand on it, and drew a bow across the strings; the granules started moving on to those parts of the plate free from vibrations, thus forming a series of attractive patterns. Plants, too, react to music. Try playing Bach's Brandenburg Concertos to your geraniums and you may win first prizes in all the Flower Shows.

The worst that can befall a music-lover, surely, is to become deaf – especially the kind of man who, on hearing a soprano singing in her bath, puts his ear to the keyhole. It was being unable to listen to opera that a certain Berliner in the 1820s regretted most when he lost his hearing. He went to one expensive specialist after another, seeking a cure. All took his money but shook their heads, until at last one said: 'They're performing Spontini's *Olympia* tomorrow at the Opera. I'm going and I have a spare seat. Why don't you come with me?'

'A waste of time,' objected the patient.

'I don't agree,' insisted the other. 'Even if you're unable to hear a note, you'll enjoy the colourful spectacle.'

They went, but although they had front row seats, the deaf man was unable to hear till, after a thunderous finale, he cried with delight: 'Doctor, a miracle – I can hear! You've cured me!' But there came no response from his companion. The explosion of sound had rendered him stone deaf.

'*You swine, you know I can't say no to Paganini!*'

Acknowledgements

Thanks are due to the following for permission to quote from the works mentioned: the authors for *Gentlemen, More Dolce Please* by Harry Ellis Dickson and *The Orchestra Speaks* by Bernard Shore; the publishers for *Friends and Fiddlers* by Catherine Drinker Bowen (Little, Brown, Boston), *My Life and Music* by Artur Schnabel (Colin Smythe), *Raggle-Taggle* by Walter Starkie (John Murray) and *A Mingled Chime* by Sir Thomas Beecham (Hutchinson); and Times Newspapers Ltd. for reviews by Ernest Newman.

The author and publishers wish to thank the following for permission to reproduce illustrations: Dobson Books Ltd, *The Hoffnung Music Festival* (1956), pages 42 and 117; Mary Evans Picture Library, page 56 (Sir Henry Wood); George G.. Harrap & Co Ltd, *Caught in the Act* (1976) with illustrations by Nerman, pages 37 (Leopold Stokowski) and 51 (Arturo Toscanini); John Murray Publishers Ltd, *Signs of the Times* by Osbert Lancaster (1961), page 60; Punch Picture Library, pages 9, 61, 63, 87, 97, 100, 144 and 146; Royal Opera House Covent Garden Archives, pages 3, 73, and 142 (*About the House*, illustration by Norman Darling); Syndication International, pages 77, 89 and 91.